A
PRINT
PLACE
BOOK

BOYS

BOYS

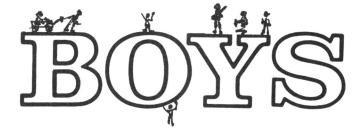

Wm Bockus, Jr

PRINT PLACE!
1943 COOLIDGE
ALTADENA·CA
91001

"THERE'S ALWAYS A SILVER LINING."

IT'S THE ROARING TWENTIES AGAIN !

Eight rascals growing up in a small midwestern town. Their thoughts & their antics lead to funny and sometimes hilarious situations, which could only happen in the twenties. Unbuckled overshoes, Jitterbugging, crew cuts and bobs are the rage.

ACKNOWLEDGMENTS

Thanks for a few extra anecdotes and laughs from Lloyd Marti, Guy DeVany, Jim Laris and John Caldwell, who were once little boys also.

AND FOR YOU KIDS OVER SIXTY:

"Billy, why don't you let your hair grow long like ordinary men?" Sound familiar? Their adult friends, heroes and sometime co-conspirators drive Flints, Graham-Paiges and air- cooled Franklins. A gallon of gas is 15 cents, and sewing machines are run by foot treadles. A postage stamp is 3 cents, an Ingersol watch is a dollar and a .38 caliber revolver can be had for $1.70 from Montgomery Ward. However, at these prices it really doesn't pay to be a thief.

TO THE REAL HEROES OF LIFE

All those persons in the
whole world who help kids
develop character, kindness
and the nerve to stand up
for justice.

Why are we always searching
for those "BIG NAME" heroes
somewhere else ?

X

"NAMES HAV BEN CHANGED
TO PROTECT THE GUILTY"

P R E F U S

My dad sed I ott to keep a diry. He sed I wood giv a thowsend dolers if I had kept one. I askd him if he wood giv me a thowsend dolers if I kept one and he sed Don't be silly. I askd him if he wood giv me a hundred dolers, and he sed he wood giv me a doler for eech munth I kept it. I figerd out I wood be 93 yeers old by the time I erned a thowsend dolrs.

When I told him it wazn't much of a deel he sed I had to luk at it in the rite perspectiv. I sed what is that? He sed there are 400 millyun chinees in China & that a laberers wage was one doler a munth, whereas all I had to do was to keep a diry to get free room and food for a munth besides. I gess he won but I am Nevr going to wurk in China when I gro up.

MY DIRY

By Billy Bockus

Sep. 15 Munday

Rained today

Sep. 16 Toosday

Rained today agen. Two dogs had a fite in our frunt
yard. Mom sed isn't it awful and stayd at the window
to see how awful it was.

Sep. 19 Friday

I forgot to rite Wensday and Thersday. After school I
coodn't find any of the gang, so I went down to the
Baxter estate on German street to see if Woodrow
Baxter wanted to come out and play. The gardner let
me in the iron gate and I nocked on the back door.
Woodrow came to the door suking on a choclut. He
sed we are making fudge candy. We don't want you.
Go home. Then he shut the door. On the way home I
saw Fish on his bicycle. I told him what woodrow
sed and Fish sed lets go thro a rock thru ther
stayned glas window but I sed we better not.

Sep. 20 Saterday

Did my chors. Took out the garbage, empteed the
wastebaskets, dusted the living room, filled the

1

water pans on the back of the radiaters, mopped the kichen flor and stratend my room.Then I looked in the icebox. We were almost out of ice, so I put the ice card in the front window with the figure 100 on top. Went up to Fritz's house. His dad used to be a gymnast and built a horizontal bar in the backyard. We all fooled around on it for a while. Then Fish climbed up on the bar and sat on it. He sed watch this and throo his arms back over his head. He swung around with the bar under his knees and then let go with his legs as he came up in frunt, but he went so fast he made a half sumersalt in the air and lit on the back of his hed. He got up pretty slowly. We sat him off to one side while we did a few birds nests and toe hangs. About 5 minutes later he stood up. We asked him how he felt. He sed fine but I can't turn my head to the left.

Fritz's mother came out then and sed we shud go home for lunch. Fish never went home for lunch cuz his folks were never ther. He sat on our cistern cover until I was thru eeting. I brot him out a frozen snicker that I keep on top of the ice block in our icebox. Dad owns a wholesale grocery warehouse and we always have boxes of candy bars, blow gum and marshmello cuckys arownd. I hardly ever eet candy.

While Fish ate the snicker two little Chicadees flew down and sat on our wire clothsline. One of them swung over and hung upside down like Chicadees like to do. Fish sed, I wonder if he can turn his hed to the left. We both laffed at that one.

I started a paper match book colection. I have one from the Nicolett Hotel in Mineapolis and one from the Palmer House in Chicago. My best and farthest one is from Roy's Gas Station in Imperial Nebraska. It has a nakid lady on the back.

Sep. 21 Sunday

Went to Sunday scool. Our class meets in the basement. The ministers wife is our teecher. We got ther kind of erly. Fish climd up into one of the cubords over the counter and puled the door shut. After a while the rest of the guys got ther and the ministers wife, Mrs. Younger, told about a guy named Saul being let down a wall in a basket or something.

Every now and then Fish wood open the cubord door and look out with a silly grin and his eyes crossed at the kids siting across the table from Mrs. Younger. They wud practicly bust trying not to laff. Finally they all burst out laffing like mad. Mrs. Younger thot they were laffing at her and stomped out saying that was the last time she was going to teach that class. She is the forth teecher to give up.

After Sunday scool we wrestld on the lawn and I got green stanes on the knees of my white pants.

Sep. 22,23,24 Mon. Toosday, Wensday

Scool, scool,scool. I cawt it on Wensday. In grammer class you can put your knee on the wood shelf under the desk and when you swing yur foot forwerd yur toe goes thru the slit between the back of the seet in front of you and the fold down seet, so you can kick the butt of the person in frunt of you without anyone seeing you. Loretta Glaser sits in frunt of me. She took about ten kicks and then she turned around and hit me over the hed with her book. Miss Gunde came down the ile, grabed me and shook me for quite a while.I am not going to try that agen.

Girls are funny. They always have to tell the teecher. If Fish was sitting ther he wud have grabbed my toe on about the third kick and twisted it and Miss Gunde woodn't have known. I have to rite the scout

3

laws 10 times and underline curteus on each one. When Miss Gunde starts the class she opens the grammer book and says, "Now where was we?" Even I kno beter than that. I shud hav her rite, Now where were we. 10 times and make her underline were each time. I gess shes getting kind of old and tired, so who cares anyway ?

Sep. 25 Thursday

After scool, me, Bunny, Goose, Tac and Fish cut sum Hollyhock stems and laid them in Gooses chicken house to dry. Goose gets his name cuz his mom raises geese, chickens and ducks. And do they stink! If you get within 100 feet of ther yard and keep breething you are a goner.

We played tipity can for a while. Babe got hit in the face with the can when his brother, Bunny knoked it off the stump before Babe cud count him out. They fawt for about 10 minutes. Bunny is older, but Babe is bigger. Babe got a bloody nose, but he ripped Bunnys shirt off.

Sep. 26 Friday

Me and Fish made a cupple of Tic Tacs after scool. You cut notches in the rims of wooden thread spools and wind string arownd the spool. Then you put a big nail thru the hole in the spool. You hold the end of the nail, put the spool agenst a window pane and pull the string hard. It makes a loud rattling sound and scares the wits out of the peeple inside.

We knew that a high school girl was baby sitting at the Kemskis this evening. After dark we sneaked up to the Kempskis and tictaked the window and ran and hid in the weeds in the empty lot next door. Well the girl opened the window and yelled out in the dark. Billy Bockus and Richard Fisher, if you wake the baby I'm going to call your folks. We cudn't figger out how she knew it was us.

Sep. 27 Saterday

Did my chores. Me, Fish, Windshield (his name is reely Winfield) Tac and Loyd hiked out to Swallows Cliff by the Cottonwood River. The Chicago Northwestern railroad trestle crosses the Cottonwood just below the cliff. Loyd thot up a fun trick. We walked out on the trestle just before the 3 o'clock freight came along and sat on the ties until the freight came arownd the bend. Then we all lowered ourselves over the edge and hung from the end of the ties. The engineer saw us on the trestle and blew his whistle like mad but he cudn't bring the freight to a stop in time, so it thundered right on over us. What we didn't figger on was how the trestle rattled and shook the ties up and down and how the engine shot out steem sideways. I was scared I was going to let go and get killed. Just then Tac lost his grip and down he went. My god I thot that was the end of him. But he was lucky. He lit smak dab in the middle of the river and went swirling downstreem until he banged into a sand bar.

Now the rest of us weren't exactly safe yet. The train stopped about a quarter mile down the track and the fireman and engineer came running back toward us. I had a heck of a time trying to pull myself back up. I finally swung one leg up on the next tie when Loyd reached down, grabbed the back of my coller and pulled me up. Loyd is older than us and is a good gymnast. He just chinned himself up. Anyhow we all ran off the trestle, down the bank to the river, dragged Tac off the sand bank and hid in the woods. We were all soaked to the waist. That was the dumbest thing we did in a long time. Tac told his mother he fell in the river.

Sep. 28 Sunday

Got anuther new Sunday Scool teecher. She is sort of fat and has a pug on top of her head. She sat down and sed "Now lets see, where are we." JR sed,"We're in the basement of a church on 4th south and Broadway." That didn't sit too well. Anyhow she read sum more about Saul and things were going ok. JR was sitting in a chair at the end of the table near the door, and when she had her nose in the book he slid out of his seat and hid under the sink. All of a sudden she noticed JR was missing. She looked under the table and then went to the door and looked up and down the hall. Then she walked down the hall. In the meantime JR got back into his chair. She comes back to the door, grabs JR by the ear and marches him away. Tac had a ping pong ball and we found sum soda straws in the cupbord. We each had a straw and tried to blow the ball past one of the guys sitting around the table. She came back to the door and stood ther. We all looked at her with the straws stiking out of our mouths. She just walked away. We kept on playing until we herd footsteps upstairs as everybody was leaving.

I have this feeling that none of us are ever going to get to heaven.

I'm sort of sick of riting every nite. Dad gave me a doler for September. I may rite sum more when I need anuther doler.
################

6

Dec. 1 Wensday

I need anuther doler. After scool me, Bunny, Tac, Goose, Fish, & Fritz checked out the Hollyhock stems at Gooses. They were nice and dry. We decided to meet inside the big lilac & spyrea bush clump in our back yard after supper. Goose brought the matches cuz his mom keeps sum by the wood heater in the chicken house and she doesn't miss them. We draw straws to see who has to smoke the first one. I lost so I had to smoke the first one. We have tried corn silk wrapped in toilet paper, dried boat oakum wrapped in brown wrapping paper, crumpled Willow bark and crumbled dried Elm leaves rolled in newspaper. Oakum was the worst. When Windshield lost and smoked the first oakum cigarette he puked. We figgerd it must have been the creosote.

I held a match to the end of the Hollyhock stem and sucked. Holy smokes, the flame came rite thru the stem like a blow torch and burnt a hole in the end of my tung. I scrambled out of the bush and ran for the hose at the back of the house. The other guys thot sumbody had cawt us smoking, so they all piled out and ran like the devil. Fish forgot the wire clothsline was ther. It caught him across the forehed, his feet went out from under him and he lit on the back of his hed agen. When we finally got back together and I had run about 10 gallons of water over my tung, we laid Fish under the Lilac bush. He came to in a minute and sed, Gee, I can turn my head to the left agen. So, you see, there's always a silver lining. If I hadn't burnt a hole in my tung, Fish might never have been able to look to the left agen.

Dec. 2 Thersday

Snowed all last night about 6 inches real soggy and made great snowballs. At scool we all go home for

7

lunch at noon and the scool doors stay locked until 1:20. The girls all gather arownd the front doors about 1:15 and shriek and screem while we guys throw snowballs at them. Today we guys made a half circle with our elbows locked together and started to push the girls against the doors. I was shoving and sliding arowned when the guys on either side of me let go, but I kept on shoving. I wasn't getting anywhere when I looked up. I was shoving against Harry Daggert, the principal. He wasn't laffing. In fact, he was sort of shaking altho I didn't think it was that cold out. He grabbed me by the sholders, put his face down by mine and sed Persons like you are the cerse of civilizishun and don't you enter those portals until every last student is inside. You got that? I sed "Yes, sir, what are portals?" He sed My God and went inside.

Dec. 3   Friday

Sun came out and all the snow melted. It usually does at first cuz the ground is so warm. After school me, Fish & Fritz went down to the humping yard by the Northwestern depot. When they switch box cars to make up diferent trains the engineer pushes the cars over a hump in the yard. Then the cars roll down the other side of the hump under their own momentum and get switched onto diferent spur tracks where they are hooked together later and pulled away by an engine. This humping saves a lot of back & forth hauling by the switch engine.

You can get some pretty long rides if you wait in the bushes by the start of the spurs. As the cars come along you run alongside and then jump on the ladder at the frunt of the car. Never jump on the ladder at the back of the car cuz if you miss, yur legs swing around between the cars and you will get yur legs cut off. If you miss at the front of the car you just bang into the side of the car and bounce off into the cinders. You get pretty scrached up but you still have yur legs.

We got about 6 rides apeece and wood have had more, but Fritz ran out from behind the bushes before the engine backed down behind the hump and the engineer saw him. Pretty soon one of the brakemen came yelling down the tracks and we took off.

We went over to the dump by the Eagle Flour Mill and threw rocks at the rats for a while. Fritz's dad works in the office at the mill, so we went over there to see if we could get a ride home. His dad sed ok so we went out to watch the warehouse men stack the flour saks in the warehouse. The floor is like polished glass from dragging the saks over it. We asked one of the men why there was chicken wire around sum of the stacks of saks, and he sed that was to keep the rats out. Then we sed why didn't those stacks have the mesh around them and he sed, "Oh, that's the white flour. Rats won't eat white flour." Isn't that funny ?

Dec. 4 Saterday

I've been taking piano lessons for about a yeer and I know 2 scales, C & F cuz F only has one black key, B flat, which makes it easy. Miss Christiansen my teecher sed I am not practising enuf. She is rite. There is an easy way to practis and still reed a book. I put a book over the music and play the scales with my left hand while I reed "Princess of Mars". When I heer mother coming from the kichen I hide the book under the music and reely try to reed the music until she goes back to the kichen.

ε music. John Carter the hero on Mars is from erth and he can jump over ten pianos end to end cuz his erth mussels are much stronger in Mars weak gravity. His girl, Dejah Thoris, is Princess of Helium. She is gorjus but keeps getting kidnaped and put in places like the Carrion Caves, The Valley of the Dead and the Tempul of Issus so Mr. Carter duzent see much of her.

His friend Tars Tarkus has 4 arms, is 8 feet tall and is green. I bet he cud play the Little Elfins March with one hand and kill a great white ape with the other three. Tars has a Thoat. It has six legs and can gallop silently over the dead sea bottoms. Miss Thoris was hatched from a pod.

Dec. 6 Munday

In science class today we made microscopes. We all brought a wooden spool. We painted the inside black with india ink. Mr. Renner gave us a piece of clear celuloid which we glued over one end. On the other end we glued a piece of thin black cardbord and made a tiny hole in the middle with a needle. Now you can put a small object like a grain of salt or a fly's wing on the celuloid and look at it thru the pinhole. It looks real big. If the sun isn't shining you can use a flashlite. Mr. Renner cut some spools in half and it made things look even larger.

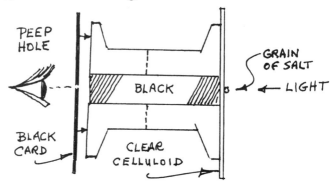

Dec. 7 Toosday

Today we looked at sum mother of vinegar thru the microscopes, and we cud see lots of wiggling little worms. Ick. I never want to eat vinegar salad dressing agen. Mr. Renner had soaked sum old hay in water for several days and we cud see more little worms darting every which way in the drop of water. He sed they were infusoria. He sure is smart.

Dec. 12 Sunday

Went to Sunday school. We didn't have a new teacher cuz we rehearsed for the Christmas program. Me, Fish and Fritz are the three Wise Men. We cum on stage from the side door and lay our gifts down by the manger where baby jesus is. Then we face the choir with our backs to the audience while the choir sings "O Little Town of Bethlehem". In the front row of the choir is Peggy. When her folks play bridge with my folks we two have to baby sit her two younger brothers, Dicky & Georgy. We turn all the lights off and lie on the floor in the dark and listen to "Inner Sanctum", Amos & Andy and "The Step on the Stairs" Peggy says we three look dumb standing there.

The second Sunday night of each month we have to go to a student bible class in the basement of the church. We sit in a circle in the dark while our minister reads the bible and then asks questions. He has a candle. Tonite I was leaning back in my chair when suddenly I went over backward. I throo out my arm sideways, grabbed the chair and did a backward summersault holding the chair in the air without a noise and got back in the circle without Reverend Younger missing a word about Saul getting let down that wall in a basket. I figgered it has been 3 weeks since he started down that wall. Fish was sitting next to me. He whispered, "That was some trick." "But why ?"

Dec. 13 Munday

Was a real warm day. Sun was out and the snow was melting. We put twigs in the gutter water and watched them run thru the pools and little ice caves all the way down to Broadway from State Street. Winshield, JR and Bunny throo snowballs on the roof of Henrietta Gorshams house. She is kind of funny in the head. She brot out her box of rocks and pegged rocks at us while she cersed us. Boy, can she cuss. She yelled a cupple of words we didn't know what they ment. When Fish told us what they ment we didn't believe him. Winshield sed, "Bull. My mother and father wud never do that." I didn't think so either.

Dec. 14 Toosday

On a lot kitty-corner frum the school they are expanding the bowling alley a cupple of lanes. They've been compacting the dirt with a big pile driver. When they took the pile driver away they left the iron weight standing near the sidewalk. Its about 7 feet tall and 18 inches square. During recess one of the north side kids bet me two bits I cudn't push it over. It looked so top heavy I shook hands on it.

I brushed sum of the sleet crust off one side; put my shoulder agenst it; braced my feet against sum ice ridges and pushed... and pushed...and pushed! It was like pushing against a house. Not a hair wud it budge. Ugh! The kid laffed and sed, Don't worry. You can get your money back tomorrow. The forman told me it weighed 2 tons and is frozen in the ground besides. I've made two and a half bucks already." Live and learn.

Dad has this old 4-cylinder white Buick runabout with a single rumbleseat facing backwards. Dad took me, in the rumbleseat, and a friend of his,Homer Skinner, out for a drive toward Sleepy Eye after work. On the way home the motor started missing and finally stopped. This is the first car dad ever had, so he knows it pretty well. He undid the leather straps and took the engine hood off and discovered that the trubble was in the distributor box. The number 2 and 4 contact springs were rusted and wouldn't make contact. They had me squat between the fender and the engine and showed me how to tap the numbers 2 & 4 in rhythm with the numbers 1 & 3 contacts. Homer cranked the engine over while dad advanced the spark slowly until I got the rhythm to keep it idling. Then Homer went around in back and pushed while dad let the clutch out easy like. We gradually got going about 10 miles per hour with me concentrating on the 1,3,2,4 / 1,3,2,4 / taca taca/ taca taca, etc. As I got the rythm, dad advanced the gas lever and we started flying. Homer lost his grip and fell down in the slush and then couldn't catch up with us. Dad yelled We can't stop now...I'll come back and get you later, and away we flew. Dad says you can always make these old cars run with a little ingenuity, but the new ones got everything covered up, and if something goes haywire, you are dead in the water. Homer was not pleased.

Dec. 15 Wenesday

Father Schreiber is a young priest at the Catholic church on south Minnesota St. On Wensday evenings he often drops into Eibner's Cafe & Bakery about 9 o'clock where Tom, our gymnastic coach, and us kids go after working out with the business men's evening gym class. He and Tom are friends and sometimes play chess while we kids kid around and eat our sundays or malts.

Tom's whole name is Thomas Paine Fender. Tom is sort of a free thinker like The real Thomas Paine was and also an evolutionist. Tonite they got discussing the origin of mankind with Tom sort of on Darwin's side and Father Schreiber on the Biblical theory that man was created instantaneously in the Garden of Eden. They got going pretty hot and heavy for about ten minutes. The discushun started becoming an argument when suddenly Fish pops out with, "This is boring! I think you guys are stupid!" (Leave it to Fish) Schreiber was sort of aghast at this upstart kid interupting their hikaflutin discushun, but Tom knows Fish and said, "OK Fish. Proceed." Fish says,"What diference does it make wether we were created quikly 6000 years ago or slowly over 6 millyon years? I would say that the fact that we're here at all is one heck of a production by somebody who wouldn't care one way or the other what conclushun you guys reech."

We kids sat looking at them. Sudenly they both laffed and Tom said, Roy, I think we better stick to chess. Then Roy said, "I've been beerded in my own den." He is a nice guy and didn't get mad at Fish like a lot of teechers would have.

Walking home I told Fish that I didn't know he cared that much about religion. He said, "I don't. But I was afraid they were going to end up mad at each other, and that would spoil our Wensday nights. So I decided to sacrifice myself and throw a monkey wrench at 'em ....eh, eh, eh."

Made a doller today at recess before sum of the suckers told everybody how much the weight weighed. Dummies.

Dec. 17 Friday

Christmas vacation starts. No school for 2 weeks. Took my piano lesson after school. Miss Christensen started to laff after I playd half a page of the Little Elfin's March. She gave me a half hug and said,"You don't care much for the Little Elfin's March, do you?" I said, "No. I only memorize the keys and then pretend to read the music." She said, "Is ther any piece of music you'd like to learn to play?" I thot a moment and then said," Yes. The Twelfth Street Rag because my brother Jerry plays that on his piano accordian all the time. She said that that was one of the more difficult pieces of ragtime to play but what say we learn it? I said you really think I could do it? Can fish swim she said. I said sure and he can dive too. She laughed like mad and said, Not that Fish... a real fish and kept laughing while she rummaged around in her music file chest.

She pulled out the 12th Street Rag sheet music and laid it on the rack. I never saw so many notes and squiggles on one page in my life. Now don't throw a fit she said. I'll teach you the right hand first and later we'll memorize the left hand. Then you can throw away the music and you'll be the life of the party for the rest of your life. But remember one thing, don't let anyone ever talk you into an oncore. Then she said something else I didn't understand: "Batehoven, forgive me."

Tonite was the Christmas Program at Turner Hall. Turner Hall is sort of the town center. It is on one whole block. It has a theater with a big stage, a gymnasium, a dance hall, a bar & card room and dressing rooms. The physical education director is Tom Fender. He is also a scoutmaster, director of the state 4-H Club Camp in Northern Minnesota, chairman of the town Republican Party, atheletic director of the high school and a lot of other things.

15

He taught us guys chess, gymnastics and how to fence. The whole town thinks he is perfect. Tom puts on a program every Christmas with the physical education classes. He says he can't trust us screwballs in an act so we help back stage changing flats, pulling up the drops, hauling around props and making up the little kids. It is a lot of fun and we are pretty good, cuz we are sort of physical.

In one of the scenes there was a church up stage center and peeple were supposed to come in from the wings and slowly walk up the church steps past a begger into the church doors to the music, Ave Maria. Well, about half the crew and cast came down with the croop and there weren't enuf peeple to walk into the church, so the first ones thru the doors wud run like mad around to the wings and walk in agen. Sometimes the walkers wood start running before they got in the doors and the audience started to snicker. Then Tom noticed the begger was missing from the steps. (He had the croop too.) So Tom threw an old gunny sack over his head and limped out to sit on the church steps. But he forgot he was the one who was supposed to put on the record "Ave Maria".

He yelled in a loud whisper, "Put on the record!" Nobody heard him. So he yelled again and again. Finally he got disgusted and yelled real loud,"Put on the goddamn record." and the whole audience heard him and then they really laughed. Toots Thompson was on the switchboard and said to me,"You know, I've never heard Tom swear. But when he did, he did it in front of the whole town, in the middle of a Christmas program and on the church steps yet."

The next bloop came in the grand finale when Mr. Victor Schroeder dressed as Santa Claws was supposed to come riding in on the moon' in front of the entire cast lined up on stage. Well, someone had put a cable clamp on the safety latch holding the moon up so it woodn't swing in accidently and kill someone during rehearsals. It got jammed and we coodn't get it off. The cast sang "Santa Claws is Coming to Town" 4 times and we still coodn't launch Vic into space. Finally Vic decided to take things into his own hands. He climbed down off the moon, grabbed a handful of spot bulbs kind of frantic like from the spares box and climbed up on top of the prompters stepladder by the tormentor with his sack of presents. He throo the bulbs on the stage floor CRASH! and then jumped off the step ladder onto the stage yelling HO,HO,HO and broke his leg. When he rolled over holding his leg the little kids all cringed back and started to cry. It was awful. The older girls ran here and there trying to comfort the little kids and sort of got things back in order. I'll say this for Vic. He had guts. He sat up and started handing out bags of candy from his sack by dragging himself across the stage from kid to kid.

We finally got the curtin down to the usual thunderus applause cuz evrybody in the building has a kid in the show. When the curtin went up for the curtin call Vic was still on the floor groaning in pain with a crying kid on each arm struggling to get loose.

Dec. 18 Saterday

Dad drove me down to the tin shop to get my skates sharpened. I get them hollow ground on his emery wheel. They don't stay sharp as long as flat grinding them with a file, but for hockey you can cut the corners better. On the way home we stopped behind a lady driving a red Flint roadster at Main and Center. There was no traffic and when she didn't move, dad honked his horn. Still she didn't turn, and dad honked a cupple more times. Finally she turned up Center street. After half a block we passed her. Dad turned and waved and waved and smiled a big smile at her. Her face changed from a mad glare to a sort of a smile and she waved back. I sed, "Who was that?" and dad sed,"I don't know." Then why did you wave, I sed. Dad sed,"Well, when we turned the corner I saw that Jay Stern had been patting a dog right in frunt of her radiator, and she cudn't move or she wood have run over him. I didn't want her to think I was an ill-mannered boor, so I pretended to be a friend honking at her." My dad is sure smart. Jay is retarded and sort of wanders around town standing on street corners smiling and waving at everybody.

This evening Fish and me went to see the Phantom of the Opera with Lon Chaney. It got out about 9 o'clock. Boy, was it spooky going home in the dark. We walked in the middle of the streets in the slush so we woodn't have to pass too close to the big snow banks by the alleys. At the end of Minnesota street was the iron railing by Oswald's foto studio. We got to arguing about wether you cud tuch yur tung on the railing real quik without it getting froze to the railing. I sed you cud. Fish sed you cudn't. So I bent over and fliked my tung at the railing. It froze tite alrite, and as I jerked up I tore a peece of skin off the tip of my tung. Cripes, did that hurt. Fish sed I told you so and you better lean over so you don't get blood on yur sheepskin coller. I grabed a wad of snow and jammed it in my mouth. It stopped bleeding pretty quik. We looked at the little white circle of skin on the railing. Fish sed it was probably the scar tisse from the Hollyhock burn on my tung and that's why it didn't bleed any worse. You see, ther's always a silver lining.

18

Dec. 19 Sunday

This afternoon Bunny, Babe, Fish, Fritz and me skiid out to Vetters Hill. The hill is about 3 blocks long and pretty wide at the top. There are 3 humps on it and the last one has a real steep slope on the down side. There are two barbed wire pasture fences that come together at the bottom and form a long narrow path for another block or so of flat run over a meadow. So you have to hit that opening which is about 20 feet wide or you end up draped over one of the barbed wire fences. The rule is that if you figger you are not going to make the opening you fall sideways and just take it, cuz the last hump is so steep on the bottom ther is no way you can brake to a stop. We guys kno that you never sit down between yur skiis to stop or slow yourself down becauz the snow gets blown away here and ther and exposes small stumps or branches and rocks frozen in the ground. In fact, our skiis have deep grooves and slivers of wood all over the bottoms from sliding over rubble and sleet ice. Vetter's Hill is no resort run.

Anyhow, we no sooner got in a cupple of runs than Fritz came schussing too fast over the last hump and made a mistake. He sat down and hit a rock frozen in the ground with his tail bone. He went rolling over and over all the way to the bottom where he laid groning. One of his skiis went sailing off under the fence and went about half a mile over the meadow. We got him up but he he cudn't walk and was groning like mad. We tied five skiis together like a tobogan, laid him on it and pulled him home. His mom called the hospital, which is rite across the street, and they brought over a strecher and took Fritz over ther.

Dec. 20 Munday

No school today...vacation. The gang sort of moped around. We went around the hospital until we cud see Fritz. He waved to us from his window. At leest he was alive. So we built a cupple of snow forts on the hospital grounds oposit his window so he cud watch us. and made a whole bunch of snowballs. Then we had a snowball fite. Pat McHale, one of my brother's frends from college, came over to watch. Then he got in the fort with us and started throwing with the rest of us, but he hardly got in the fort when he raised his head above our fort and a snowball hit him rite between the eyes. He went home then. You never raise yur hed above the fort when Fish is on the other side. You look throo one of the peepholes first and then raise up and throw because Fish has a habit of throing his snowballs as hard as he can just over the top of your fort agen and agen as he figgers sooner or later one of the guys will stick his hed up just as the snowball arrives. We figgered Pat had enuf sense to remember that, but I gess not. Then we got to making too much noise and Dubby Dubby Dobrens, the hospital janitor, came out and chased us away.

Dec. 21 Toosday

Fritz's mother sed it was ok to go see Fritz. So in the afternoon we all went to the hospital. He was lying in bed and sed he cud feel his toes now. Doctor Howard told him the X-rays showed nothing broken but he was going to be eating his meals standing up for some time. That sure was good news. That accident sort of took the fun out of the gang. You kno sumthing? You can't be happy yourself unless the peeple around you are happy too.

Doc Howard is a neat guy. He can throw a football a block, and the front point of the football follows an arc and is pointing down toward the receever when it lands. When we guys throw it, it sort of points up and mushes down sideways. He is pretty smart too. Dad sed that Doc Howard was out doing his weekly clinic at the poor farm and noticed that the little girl of the manager was going blind. He did sum reserch and telefoned experts all over the United States and finally figgered out what was wrong with the little girl. Then he used his own money and sent her to a clinic in New York and now she can see agen. At Christmas time he goes throo all the bills of the poor peeple, marks them paid, and sends them out with his Christmas cards.

He lives next door to us. Sometimes he gets so tired he comes over to our house, slumps down in the easy chair in our sunroom and goes to sleep. When he does that, mother won't answer the phone until he wakes up. After about an hour he'll wake up and tear off on his calls agen. He's a bachelor. Sometimes he walks in about suppertime and just sits down at our table, and dad serves him just as if he was one of the family and ate ther all the time. He can put a whole boiled potato in his mouth and pretend to be a gorilla. When he's around, everybody seems happy and laughing and excited or something. I hope I'm like that when I grow up.

Dec. 22 Wensday

Started to blow last nite and had a blizzard all day today. About 3 o'clock the wind died down to about 20 miles per hour and it stopped snowing, but when the sun went down about 4, the thermometer on our back porch dropped to 40 below. Tac had called to see if I wanted to ski some before supper and mom sed Yes, but I don't think you'll last very long. I sed, Pooh,Pooh I've never been cold. I even loan my fur mitts to other guys and wear their frozen ones until they are thawed out. Once I even changed mocassins and socks with Goose when we got a cupple of miles beyond Camel's Back and he cudn't feel his toes. Anyhow, I put on my long underwear, two pair of wool socks, my sheepskin snow packs and over those my leather mocassins. I had a brown wool army shirt and my sheepskin coat with a scarf around my face and my wool lined leather ski helmet tied under my chin. As I put on my wool knit mitts and a pair of furlined mittens with elastic cuffs, mother sed, "Are you sure you can walk?"

I crunched out to the garage, picked up my skiis and met Tac in the middle of the street. Ther wuzn't a car moving anywher. We skiid down the middle of the street out to the gravel pits at the edge of town. Ther were a zillion stars overhead and it was absolutely quiet. We cud hear sum dog barking down in Walahi. We pushed over the edge of the pits and skiid down out on the flats. About a mile further the innertube rubber bands we use to help keep our skiis on just cracked and fell off. We crossed the flats and started over "The Bogs". which are sort of big grass bumps that swell up in the swamp just below Vetters Hill. We were watching the time, cuz we figgered 40 minutes out and 40 minutes back wud get us back in time for supper ok. But now the wind started up again. It started gusting and I was getting colder and colder. We both took a pee, cuz they say ther is no sense in trying to keep all that pee warm, as your body will do. Then Tac sed, "I'm freezing to death." We turned around and started back, but now the wind was in our faces and was reely blowing. I started shaking and Tac sed, Do you think we're going to make it? I sed sure but we better hurry.

Finally we got back to the bottom of the gravel pits and up on top were dad and Tac's dad on skiis waiting for us. We carried our skiis and hiked up to them. We were so cold we cud hardly talk and were shaking like mad. They sed they noticed when the wind started that they better cum after us and were just getting ready to follow our tracks when we showed up. When we got in the house, I finally stopped shaking and drank some cocoa. Dad said to mom, "Why did you let them go?" Mom just laughed and said, "It gives them character. And besides I knew they wudn't get too far at 40 below." It's sort of funny, but I've noticed that dad usually worries more about us kids than mom does.

Tomorrow is the Christmas Program at church. I hate Christmas Programs. When I'm in one I always feel uneasy. I'll be playing and having fun and all of a sudden I'll think Christmas Program and I get that uneasy feeling all over agen. Sometimes adults don't know anything about kids!

Dec. 23 Thursday

I felt uneasy all day. Like Tars Tarkus who could sort of sense the future, I had this feeling of impending doom, but then Fritz came home from the hospital and made it to the Christmas program ok, so I forgot about it.

We got to the church at 6 to get made up. There were a lot of little kids running around and several girls putting makeup on them or helping people put on their costumes. We got into our robes and a lady put on our gray wigs and bustled around and told us to sit quiet until we were called, which we did for once. Willie, the ministers son, came over and looked at us and said, "What have you got on under the robes?" Fritz said, "Nuthin." So then Willi started yelling, "The wise men are nakid, The wisemen are nakid." Fish started after him, but he ran away. A lot of the girls were laffing at us.

The lady finally called us to go on. We wood have been ok, but ther was a mirror in the hallway on the way to the stage and when we looked in it we looked like 3 little old ladies. Espeshally Fritz who wore glasses with thin brass rims. We started to laugh, and couldn't stop. Then the door opened and we marched across the stage and put the Frank Insense and Moor by the manger. Then we faced the girls in the choir.

We were laffing so hard the tears were streeming down our faces but we didn't care cuz the audience coodn't see our faces anyhow. But now the girls in the choir took one look at us and started to choke. They screwed up ther faces to keep from laffing and coffed and used ther hankerchiffs to blow ther nose. Peggy Swartz was pretty smart. She dropped her hymn book behind the little curtin in front of the choir. The curtin is ther so the audience can't see the girls legs. She bent over to pick up her book but you cud see her sholders heeving up and down while she reely let go laffing. When she did sit up agen her eyes were wide and her mouth was set sort of funny. Then two other girls dropped ther books. Plop, plop. That did it. The entire choir gave up. They just didn't giggle, they guffawed, howled, and roared until then the audience started to laugh. We turned to see what they were laffing at, and then the audience laffed harder than ever.

Miss Stolz walked up on the stage. She was laffing too. She stood on the edge of the stage and sed, Well, you kno, I believe that was the best scene we ever put on. Becawz, isn't Christmas the time for joy? Then the audience started clapping and there were even a few whistles. It was bedlam. Me, Fish and Fritz snuk back to the basement. We thot we were going to catch it for sure, but Miss Stolz came over and sed, Don't worry boys, that was the funniest dam act I've ever seen. She even sed dam.

Dad drove us home and he didn't even say a word but evry time he looked at us he wood bust out laffing. When we got home dad showed me the evening paper. Two men were found this morning frozen to death on the Minnesota River flats about 3 miles out of town. I gess Tac and me were lucky. I'm sure not going to pooh pooh winter anymore. Christmas eve tomoro.

Dec. 24 Friday

The river is frozen over now. The blizzard blew a lot of the snow off the ice so Goose, Bunny & Babe, Tac, Windshield, JR, and Fish and I went down to the river with Ed Hagen. Ed is older than us. He is in college, but when he comes home he plays hockey with us and is not snooty. Once he drove five of us over to see a night football game at Gustavus Adolphus college in St. Peter. There was a big bonfire before the game and we lerned one of the yells.

Rootity toot, Rootity toot
We're the boys from the Institute
We don't drink and we don't chew.
We swallow teams from Hamlin U
WHOLE !

We all put on our skates. Then we all went out about 40 feet from shore and at a signal from Ed we all jumped up at once and came back down hard on the ice. If the ice had broken it wouldn't hav been a good idea to skate that day. But it didn't. All we herd was a loud CRACK and a smaller one, crack but those are just long fissure cracks that radiate out from a pounding in cold weather. Ed carried a coil of rope around his waist and made us skate in pairs. Then in case someone breaks thru, his buddy lies down quik to distribute his weight on the ice and waits until Ed gets ther with the rope, but nobody did.

Anyhow the ice is usually real thick by Christmas. In February the ice company uses a big circular saw to cut cubes of ice out of the river and then stores them in sawdust in a big barn for use in iceboxes during the summer.

We skated a cupple of miles up river against the wind. Then we turned around and held our coats wide open with both arms. The wind wood get you going strate ahead about 15 but when you went sideways you could tear along about 30 mph from bank to bank. That was reely fun. Ed said that was reaching. The last run back we had a race. Ed won but I was second. You kno why? Becuz I borrowed my sister, Charlottes sheepskin coat which is too big for me but I knew it wood make a heck of a sail. Nobody even noticed it buttoned on the left side.

Dec 25 Saterdy

Christmas morning. Jerry was home from the university of Minnesota and we all opened presents. I got new   FLEXIBLE FLYER sled. Boy, what a beauty. I got a Lionel electric train, a pair of new fur mitts, a pair of leather boots with a jack knife stuck in a pocket on the side of the right boot and six books. They are:

Tarzan the Terrible	The Warlord of Mars
Tarzan and the Jewels of Opar	At the Earth's Core
The Gods of Mars	The Moon Maid

Dec. 26 Sunday

Red the two mars books.

Dec. 27 Monday

Red the Moon Maid. Julian the 6th, Julian the 9th and Red Hawk is the hero. He is reincarnated 3 times. His girl friend is Nah-ee-lah on the moon; Juana in the Chicago teivos and Bethelda in the desert. Orthis is the mad scientist who helps the Kalkars from the inside of the moon invade Erth in 2056. Kalkars have 4 legs, low foreheads, pointed ears and never smile. Orthis invents an electric weapon that can disintegrate metal on the Erth's flying vessels, but Julian paints his flagship with a gray insulating paint and foils Orthis. Of course Erth is by now smashed to pieces and the peeple have become sort of like indians, but with Orthis dead, Julian and his tribes manage to drive the Kalkars into the Pacific Ocean where they take off into the sunset. Then he took Bethelda into his arms and covered her mouth with kisses.

Went around to the other guys houses to see what they got. JR got a Benjamin Pump Air Rifle. The more pumps of air you put in the farther the BB goes. Bunny & Babe got an airdale puppy. They named it Pal. Ther dad got the family a new Franklin car that doesn't have a radiater. It is aircooled and the front slants backward like a Graham-Paige, reely modern.

Went to Fish's. When I got ther he had alredy taken apart a toy submarine, a dancing minstrel man, a tin music box and a two-foot long wooden batleship that fired wooden bullets. He had all the parts laid out on newspaper on the kichin table. He put each toy back together for me and then took them apart agen. When we got redy to leev he carried the newspaper into his bedroom, opened the botom drawer of his dreser and dumped all the parts into it. The drawer was alredy haf ful of cog wheels, axels, cotter pins, tires and all kinds of peeces of toys. He is so nuts about taking things apart that he carrys a little tool with him all the time. It's a screwdriver on one end, a file and small hack saw on the side & an adjustible rench on the other end.

Dec. 28 Toosday

Mom has ben reeding my diry and showing me how to spell sum words. Tuesday, Wdnesday, really, teacher, throw and could or would are sum some of them. I told her I thot my way was better. Take rough, cough, through and though. They are spelled the same and pronownced different. I sed that is dum and she sed yes it is. And I sed why don't they change and spell like I do? And she sed, "Many peeple are yeers ahed of sosietys tradishuns but thers always a lag before common sense prevales. Most scool children accept the regular spelling without questuning it at all. You are much more observing and inteligent than most peeple. Never forget that." I sed, "If I'm so smart why don't I get all A's in scool?" "You will," she sed "but yur not reddy yet." Boy, mom can sure make you feel good. I alway thot I was sort of dum geting mostly C's all the time. I ~~reely~~ really felt great all day.

Dec. 29 Wednesday

Fish and I have a neat trick. We pulled it off agen this afternoon. The door to the Turner Hall gym opens on a balcony above the gym floor. The railing is an old wood one with initials carved in it and about 10 coats of gray paint on it. We waited outside until a cupple of girls started to go in. They were Gretchen and Kathy. We started to open the door for them but pretended it was stuck. Then I step back, and give it a shove with my sholder. It flys open and I go skidding across the balcony as if I'm slipping, grab the railing and cartwheel over it with my sheepskin flapping and my overshoes sailing over the rail. But I grab the botom rail and the edge of the balcony to stop me sumwhat and drop to the flor on my feet with a loud BANG. Then I laid down quiklike on my back with my eyes wide open as if I'm dead. In the meentime Fish sort of gets in the way of the girls so they don't get to the railing too quik to see me lay down. They looked over the rail and sed, "My god, what happened. Did he slip?" Then they and Fish ran down the stares over to my body. When they bent over me I kept staring at the ceiling like a stiff. Fish sed, "I'll get a doctor." and ran up the stares.

Tom Fender was sitting in his office at the end of the balcony, typing, and he yells out, "Billy, you're going to snap yur spine doing that gag sumday, so knock it off!" I looked at the girls and stuck out my tung. They rolled thei eyes up and Gretchen sed, "Bill, you're crazy. I shud have known better!" I looked up at her and thought... She sure is pretty. Then I realized that was the first time anybody ever called me Bill.

Just then Tom yelled,"Say, do you 4 want to go with me to Minneapolis tonite? The Chocolate Soldier is opening at the Schubert Theater." Of corse we all sed yes. He sed, Well, tell yur folks its my treet, I'll get the tickets. I'll pick you up at 5:15 if its ok with yur folks, but tell them we won't get back 'till after midnite."

After the show, Tom took us back stage. We cud see into the heroines dressing room. It was full of flowers and lots of peeple were all talking at once. When she looked up and saw Tom, she pushed thru all the peeple, ran out, gave him a hug and sed,"Thomas Fender" and gave him a pretty long kiss rite in frunt of everybody. Tom introduced us to her. She was beautiful. (Tom is pretty good looking himself.) I think her name was Marilyn Miller. Tom knows everybody.

December 30 Thursday

JR got into a mess of truble yesterday. Last September he got a job delivering The Brown County Journal newspaper when one of the delivery boys moved away. He did ok for quite a while. Then he got tired delivering papers, so each day he wood thro about 20 papers down the storm drain at the corner of fifth and State St. Of corse the peeple wood yell about not getting ther paper, but becuz of the snow and wind and cuz lots of peeple only reed the Minneapolis Tribune anyhow, ther wern't more complaints than usual.

Now JR wood have pulled it off but he made the mistake of throing all the papers down the same storm drain cuz it had a reel big opening. It thawed the last few days and the whole intersecshun got flooded about a foot deep. When the street guys checked the drain, they hawled out about a ton of soggy Brown County Journals. They told the journal and it wasn't long befor they traked down the culprit. JR told us today he was unemployed and he had to do the dishes for two months.

Dec. 31 Friday

My brother, Jerry, takes electrical engineering at the U. He skipped the 2nd and 5th grades too. He built us a radio last year. It was the first one in town. It is about 3 feet long with six dials on the frunt and it's made of bakelite, sort of a black hard rubber. Our airial is about 60 feet long with six wires and goes from the roof of our house across two empty lots to a forty-foot tower he built. You put on ear phones to hear. Tonight ther was a special program from London and you could hear the bells from Big Ben and some other stuff. We took turns on the ear phones listening just before supper.

Tonite was New Year's eve. The fireman's ball at Turner Hall is the big event and evrybody in town is ther. This is one nite all our folks let us stay out until midnite. We guys get together after supper and go up to Turner Hall about 10 o'clock. We sit on the theater steps outside and just watch. The town tuffs get pretty drunk inside and evry now and then two of them will cum out and fite in the snow. They usually take off ther soot coats and fite in ther shirtsleeves. It's bare knuckles and boy can they hit and boy can they take it too. It's splat, splat, splat and the guy's noses start to bleed and run down over ther white shirts but they don't care, they just keep socking away until one of them falls down. Sometimes they are so drunk they both fall down or get so tired they just sort of wrestle around on the sidewalk or in the snowdrifts. Then they put ther arms around each other and start crying and stagger back inside. Sometimes we have to yell at them to pick up ther soot coats and they thank us very politely.

The best fiter is Nuts Kuggameister. He usually comes out about 3 or 4 times with a different guy each time. I don't know what he does inside to make so many guys hate him, but the fites don't last very long. In fact, Nuts never even bothers to take off his soot coat. We guys think Nuts was a boxer once, because he doesn't swing his arms around like most of them do. He crouches and waits; dodges a few punches, and then snaps his left in strate a cupple of times and suddenly he will jab, jab, jab, throw a right cross and splat, the other guy will fall down on his hands and knees and slide slowly onto his face in the

31

slush. Then Nuts picks the guy up and drags him back inside so he doesn't freeze to the sidewalk. He doesn't forget to pick up the guy's soot coat either. We don't think Nuts drinks very much.

Jan. 1 Saturday
We all drove down to Minneapolis erly this morning in the Cadillac with four lap robes. Dad had put the curtains on but it gets pretty cold about the time you get to Gaylord. The Chamber of Commerce has painted yellow bands around trees and telephone poles to mark the shortest routes to Minneapolis and if you miss one of those yellow bands on the telephone poles because of some sleet crust you're apt to get lost and wander around on some back roads until a farmer tells you where to go. There were snow banks on each side of the road until we passed Gaylord. Guess the blizzard hadn't hit so hard north of us.

We always visit Grandma and Aunt Lil and take Jerry back to the U. We only had one flat just outside of Shakopee. It took us 3 1/2 hours to go the hundred miles not counting the flat, which is pretty good time. Dad said they are going to start tarring some of the roads between Glencoe and Shakopee this spring which will cut down on flat tires too.

Mom and Charlotte went down town to Dayton's Dept. Store to get Charlottes hair bobbed. Dad said it was a shame to cut off her lovely long hair but grandma said she thought Charlotte looked great. I thought so too. She is the first girl in town to get her hair bobbed.

My two little cousins, Phyllis and Jeanne came home from Sunday school Sunday morning and were running around grandma's house singing, "Onward Christian Soldiers going as to war, with the crosseyed Jesus going on before." Nobody noticed except me.

Stanley Fremgarde next door to grandma's got a crystal radio set for Christmas, but he couldn't make it work. Jerry went over Sunday and fiddled with it. He made a longer airial outside and made a better ground by putting a piece of screen door metal screen under the dirt and sprinkling it with salt to pull the moisture in and sprinkled water over it. He changed the circuit a bit and put in what he called a coil. He wrapped some of the left over copper airial wire around the inside of a toilet paper roll and connected that in the circuit with another piece of wire that Stanley could move back and forth along the coil and finally it worked great. We would move the wire and the needle back and forth and around on the crystal until you heard something in the earphone. There is only one broadcasting radio station in Minneapolis, WCCO, but I think it is really somthing to get music over the air without any telephone wires at all, just using a couple of wires and a crystal rock.

Stanley is 16 and always plays with me when I visit grandma. I like him a lot. He said Jerry was a genius. I think Stanley is a genius too.

Jan. 3 Monday

This afternoon dad took us all to the matinay at the Orpheum Theater. It was a real play called The Bat. It was scary. In one part the stage living room is empty and its thundering and litning outside. All of a sudden the bat sticks his head up from behind the davenport. He has two big fuzzy ears, two holes for a nose and fangs. He looks slowly around the living room. Just then the heroine comes on stage and the bat pulls his head down. She sits on the davenport. Up comes the the horrible head agen just behind her. Little Jeanne yells out, "Lookout behind you!" Well, the awdience lets out a few laffs and we got Jeanne shushed before she sed anything else. Just then there was a crash of thunder and the shadow of a gigantic bat is cast on the wall by a bright flash of litning. The lites go out. There's a screem. End of Act II. I kept clutching dads arm, Jeanne kept crawling into my lap but Phyllis just sat chewing her Jujus. Nothing ever scares her. Plays are sure better than movies. Boy!

Jan. 4 Tuesday

School started today agen. Thers a house in sort of a hollow at the corner of Broadway that I have to pass on the way to school. The Linders live ther and every once in a while Sonny Linder will come up the stares from his house when I'm on the way to school and shove me backwards. He says,"Whats your name, kid?" and he knows my name as well as I do. I say,"Billy." and he says,"Billy, what?" and I have to say,"Billy Bockus." and then he lets me by. He's about a head taller than me and I don't know what to do. During vacation I told Jerry about it and Jerry sed I think we can do something about this.

Jerry sed, "You know these bullies don't realy think you'll fite back and the next time he shoves you, lite into him with all you've got. Even if he licks you, you'll find he'll probably leave you alone after that. But you and I are going to have a little training period this week before you tackle him.

So Jerry started to show me a few ways to throw a punch. It was kind of the way Nuts Kuggemeister hit. Jerry sed, "First of all if you are going to fight, fight. Don't tap somebody and expect them to back off. Give it all you've got in the first few minutes and keep boring in. Expect to get hurt but figger you're going to hurt the other guy more. Now... if you don't

34

think this way then don't get into a fight in the first place because you will get murdered. Got that ?" I sed,"OK."

He showed me how to hunch my left sholder forward and straighten out my left arm with a snap while I turned my fist a quarter turn clockwise but still keeping my balance. Then we did the right arm the same way. After a few evenings he started me on a combination like left jab, left jab, and then a quick follow up with a left jab, but this time step forward to give your left jab a little more length and then throw your body with everything you've got into a right cross. And this time aim with your right fist for a spot BEHIND the guys head. This makes sure that your right arm is still slightly bent when your fist reaches his chin. Then your arm straightens and delivers the final snap, splat, and isn't wasted in the air before the fist gets ther.

Another evening he got two baseball gloves out, put one on each hand and sat on a chair. He held the glove on my right a little higher and sed, pretend this is his head. And pretend this other is his body. I would jab,jab at the left glove and and then step in with the cross to the right glove until he was satisfied I was timing it ok and getting my whole body weight into the second punch. The last thing he sed when we left him off at the university was, "And start your attack while he's talking. Cuz when people talk, their brain is thinking about talking and they react about a second slower than when they're not talking... Got it, Willy?" I sed OK. and he sed, "Go get 'em!"

Jan. 5 & 6 Wednesday & Thursday

Cold and snowing. Sonny didn't show up either day.

Jan. 7 Friday

I got into trouble agen today. Before vacation I copied Wayne Walstrups name on the side of the big dictionary in the library just like he signs it. I am pretty good at forgery. Anyhow Mr.Spietzerbach, the librarian, saw it today, came into study hall and jerked Wayne out of his desk and gave him the devil. Wayne kept saying he didn't do it, but old Spitz sed, "It's your handwriting" and shook him somemore.

I felt awful and decided to tell him it was me. I knew Old Spitz would say, "Students, this boy is a model of moral integrity. Both of you boys return to your seats. The matter is forgotten." So I walked up to him and sed, "Sir, I am the one that wrote Wayne's name on the dictionary." He dropped Wayne and grabbed me and sed,"So your the culprit." He turned me upside down, then rite side up and shook me until my teeth rattled. Then he slammed me in my desk and sed, "Persons like you make me fear for the culture of America."

He sure must like dictionaries. I guess I don't like being noble.

Jan. 8 Saturday

Played cops and robbers all day. We used our bikes in the morning. The idea is for the robber to ride away from the cops until he is out of sight and then try to get back to the intersection we call the bank within 20 minutes without getting cawt by the rest of the gang. You cannot get off and walk your bike into a hiding spot. You must keep riding on the streets or alleys. If you are spotted you can turn and try to lose any cop chasing you. The cops have to be careful not to let the robber get between them and the bank or he'll be home free. The cops carry several tennis balls and must hit the robber with a ball to capture him.

This morning I got up real erly. Mom gave me an old skirt, one of her old fur jackets and a white fur hat. I put them in a cardbord box and rode up to Turner Hall where I hid them under the steps. The gang met about 9 o'clock at 5th and State. We had a cupple of runs, but each time we cops cawt the robber. Then it was my turn to be robber. I rode down State until second south. They can't chase you until you are out of sight. Then I turned suddenly, ducked uner the Turner Hall steps, where I rolled up my pant legs, pulled on the skirt, jacket & hat. Then I rode slowly across State street going east. Fritz had been left on guard watching down State to make certain I didn't double back and cross State. He saw me but thot I was a girl. Ha, ha,ha.

It was duck soup from then on. I rode south on Broadway, back to 5th south where I turned up and rode through the bank intersection about 40 feet behind Fritz. He glanced at me but still thought I was a girl. I went over and sat on Besmehn's steps. After about ten minutes the guys all came back and stood around saying how they had outfoxed me. Then I went over to them and sed in a girl's voice, "Can you tell me if Billy Bockus is here. I think he's cute." Well, they about busted and sed it wasn't fair and made a rule right then, that after this we cudn't use disguises.

Dad sed during supper that I got in the barn before they closed the door. Whatever that meant.

After lunch we played cops and robbers on foot. The robber can tell the cops where to stand and then he runs until he's out of sight and then they can all chase after him. But this time the robber has to find a hiding place within an area two blocks on a side, so the cops can pretty well pinpoint the area he's hiding in. If they can't find him in 20 minutes, he wins. It was about 4 o'clock and pretty dark when it came my turn to be robber. I had the cops stand at 5th and State while I went down almost to 6th and State. You have to work fast cuz the guys can run a block in about 15 seconds. I ran between McHales house and Stuses to make them think I was going into that block, but I cut around the back of McHales house and ran across the street to where they were building a three story addition on the Union Hospital. I ran up to the third floor and squeezed myself down into one of the clothes chute holes and waited.

Pretty soon I herd the gang walking around and yelling to each other. When they came up to the third floor I was afraid they might see me so I slid down the chute a little farther. They couldn't see me in the dark even though I saw the head of one of the guys look down my hole. They cudn't find me and I heard ther voices geting fainter and fainter.

I managed to get my Ingersol out of my pocket and when twenty minutes had passed I started back up. But I reached a place where the tin overlapped in the chute, the edge caught my pants and I couldn't go any farther. There I was and it got colder and colder. I started yelling but my voice didn't travel very far in that clothes chute. I thought of sliding farther down, but thought that might be worse, so I stayed where I was and kept yelling my head off every few seconds.. Pretty soon I heard somebody walking around yelling. I yelled some more, and it was Dubby Dubby Dobrens the hospital janitor. He yelled back, "Keep yelling until I find you." Finally I could see his head at the top of the chute and he sed, "Are you all right ?" and I sed, "Yes, but I'm stuck." He sed wait a minute and I'll get a rope." So he let the rope down and pulled me out, but the tin ripped my pants from my belt to my ankle on the way up. He told me he had come out to the boiler

house to shake the clinkers out of the fire grate when he heard me yelling. I thanked him. I always thought he was an old grump, cuz he'd make us get off the hospital lawn when we made too much noise. But he seemed like a pretty nice guy now.

It was almost six o'clock when I got home. Mom sed, "I was getting worried. What happened ?" and I told her. She sed, "Good Lord, you were about to freeze yourself to death again?" I sed I guess so and showed her the rip in my pants. She rolled her eyes and sed, "Don't you think you ought to write Mr. Dobrens a letter?" I sed, "Gee, he probably saved my life. I can't ask him to pay for a new pair of pants." She sed, "No, you dumkopf, a letter to thank him for saving your life." So I did.

Well, that was another dumb thing I did. But I did fool the gang with my girl disguise. There's always a silver lining.

Jan. 9 Sunday

Our new Sunday school teacher is a man. His name is Jim Becher. Two of the guys were fooling around at the end of the table and Mr. Becher sed,"No!"

without even looking up and they both stopped. He is tuff. The first thing he sed was, "What did you think of the Gophers beating the Hoosiers in the last second yesterday?" Everybody sed wasn't that something! Then he asked about our hockey team. We told him how we scraped the snow off the sloo down by the Northwestern tracks and made cages out of chicken wire. We told him how we made our own water fountain after they wouldn't let us use the fountain in the depot with our skates on. We chopped a hole in the ice and whoever drinks lies down with his mouth over the hole. Then two guys jump up and down on each side of the hole and the drinker can get a good slug with each plop of water that pops out. Mr. Becher sed, "No kidding? and started to laugh like mad.

He sed, "What do you use for a puck and we told him we use a round Copenhagen Snuff box packed with some lead scraps from Gulden's plumbing shop and rapped with electrishuns tape. He asked what we used for sideboards and we sed we just banked the snow around the edge cuz boards were too expensive. He sed, "Say, I've got an idea. There's a pile of old planks lying right by the depot. You guys wait here a minute while I make a phone call to Red Pink. He's the station master." And off he went. He is the first Sunday School teacher that ever left us alone without telling us to behave while they were gone or God would strike us down from behind with a bolt of lightning.

He was back in a few minutes and sed, "Red sed to take them all and if you want to store them over the summer shuv them under the waiting room on the south side."

He got some paper and pencils out and had each of us draw a design that we thought would hold the planks upright. Then he sed, "So what do you say we all wear old clothes next Sunday and get here at 9 o'clock. Bring a hammer and any nails you can round up." When we finished the designs, Sunday school was over. He collected the papers and sed, "We'll check 'em out next time. And then we'll go down and build us a rink!"

Wow, I can hardly wait until next Sunday.

Jan. 10 Monday

Today it happened. Sonny came up his steps this morning and waited for me. My heart was beeting like mad when I saw him standing there. He came up to me and gave me a shove and sed, "What's your ... I gave him a left jab in the chest, stepped in and hit him in the face with everything I had with my right, rotating fist and everything. I was surprised. I expected him to come right back at me. Instead he fell backwards, sat down on the top of his stares and then sort of rolled backwards down the steps, thump, thump, thump. He got up, looked at me and started to bawl and ran into his house.

I ran on to school sort of shaking, wundering what he would do to me tomorro. I worried and worried all morning, until all of a sudden I thought to myself, Well, I didn't do too bad. If he comes after me tomorrow I'll just give it all I've got. If I get licked, so what, he'll know he's been in a fight, so stop worrying about that stupid bully. Then I had the funniest feeling. I kinda hoped he would try something.

When I got home after school, Mom sed that Mrs. Linder had called her that morning and gave mom the dickens because I had hit her boy. But mom sed, "I gave her a piece of my mind and told her if she'd keep her boy from shoving little kids around he wouldn't get his face punched!" That was funny, because I was wondering how mom would feel. She's always so nice to everybody. I guess she can be tough when she wants to.

Jan. 11 Tuesday

Sonny didn't show up at all.

Jan. 12 Wednesday

Our English teacher, Miss Ritter, asked us to find or make up a paragraph that would best describe a single emotion such as happiness grief, hate or whatever. I found this one in one of dad's "Crimes of Horror" stories:

"Terror, with its bloodshot eyes, lolling tongue, clawlike nails, blood congealing screech and boundless stride that takes by surprise those who were hourly expecting it."

She gave me an A on it, but seemed surprised when I told her where it came from.

It sure described how I felt going past Sonny Linder's house every morning.

Jan. 13 Thursday

On Thursday we got out early. There was some kind of a teachers meeting. Fish and I were walking along Washington street in front of Keckeisen's house when I thought a bee stung me on the leg, but then I realized it was winter. Yikes did that hurt. I started to roll up my pant leg to see what it was, when Fish jumped up in the air and yelled "OW!" He looked all around and said, "Don't look around. Just keep on walking as if nothing happened, cuz I saw someone dodge behind Schulke's garage. It's probably JR with his Benjamin pump. So we walked to the end of Washington street where it goes downhill to Wallahi. As soon as we got out of sight of JR we ran across southside park over to the hospital, around McHale's house and came up to JR's house behind some bushes. Sure enough, there was JR pumping up his gun. A mail man was delivering the mail to Keckeisen's house and as he walked up to their house, JR leaned the gun against the garage door and squeezed one off. Boy, the mailman jumped up in the air and started rubbing his butt and looking all around. But JR was back inside the garage laffing his head off. Well, the mailman left and we let JR pump the gun up once more. Then we came up behind him. Fish grabbed the gun and shot JR in the leg. JR yelped and jumped around rubbing his thigh. Then he ran for the house and yelled, "You'll be sorry. I'm going to tell my mother." I sed, "We better get out of here." Fish sed,"Don't worry. He won't tell his mother anything." I sed, "Why not?" Fish sed, "Then he has to tell how he shot us and the mailman. Shooting a mailman is a federal offense. Jr could go to jail for life." Fish knows all sorts of things. Anyhow Fish got out his little tool and took the BB gun over to a bench in the garage. He started taking it apart and I asked him what he was doing. He sed, "I'm not sure yet, but I think I can fix it so he can't get so much power out of it."

He got the parts laid out on the bench and sed, "I think I've got the answer. When the plunger is shoved in after the gun has been fired, it does two things. It shoves this cam down which closes the release valve to the pressure chamber and gets the chamber ready for the next pressure fill. It also pumps air into the chamber at the same time. On the second pump, however, the first cam has laid down and brought up the second cam. This second cam holds the release valve in place until the chamber is full. What I'm going to do is file this second cam down so it doesn't quite hold the valve shut... sort of like it was worn. Then the air will keep leaking out as he pumps and he'll never get the power out of it even with 10 pumps. And the longer he waits to shoot, after pumping it up, the weaker it will get...eh he eh... diabolical, huh?" He laid it on the bench and we left.

Loyd came up with another of his dumb tricks this evening. Spot had his dad's Stude and we were driving around looking for some girls to wave at, when suddenly the front door flew open and Loyd flew out, but he hung on to the top of the door and let his feet drag along the gravel. Then he ran along, pulled himself up on the door, jumped back in and slammed the door shut, saying, "Spot, you ought to have your dad get this door latch fixed." Very funny. The rest of us went on talking and pretended we hadn't noticed anything. He's always pulling stuff like that.

Jan. 14 Friday

The whole gang went to the movies tonight. We went to the Nile Theater to see Art Acord in the Oregon Trail. It's a serial and this was the second last episode. Fifteen cents is a lot to pay to see a serial, but the main pictures are a lot of talking and mushy love scenes with no action. Tonight we all sat in the front row and saw a Pathe Newsreel and a Charley Chase comedy before the serial came on.

Last week Art Acord walked into an Indian Rope Snare. It tightened around his ankles and when the tree sprang upright it jerked him upside down about 30 feet above the ground. On the way up his hunting knife fell out of its sheath and landed in the snow.

There he was trapped. Well, this week the serial showed us the last part of last week's action. Art gets snapped up into the air, the knife drops out of the sheath, but crime 'n ently, this time he reaches down and grabs the knife out of the air BEFORE it hits the snow. That is no fair. We all booed until Mr. Melzer, the owner, came down and shushed us up. Heck, who can't get out of an Indian rope snare if you have a knife. You just reach up, grab the rope with one hand and cut your feet loose with the other. We practically wasted our 15 cents.

Art then crawled under the ice by the river ford breathing the air between the water and the ice until the three dirty mean filthy outlaws came to the ford. Art shot two of them and finally choked the third one to death after a bloody fight in the snow. At the end of the picture we left him lying in the snow at night with a broken leg surrounded by a pack of wolves with only one bullet left in his Winchester.

But we all decided not to spend our fifteen cents on the last episode next week. Art double crossed us and now we don't give a tinker's dam what happened to him. The last episode will probably show the sun coming up, his leg healed, a full magazine in his Winchester and the wolves nothing but a team of Huskies pulling a sledge driven by a pretty girl whose father is Governor of Oregon.

There are plenty of guys like Yakima Canute, Hoot Gibson, Wallace Reid, Antonio Moreno or Tom Mix that are real heroes. We saw Antonio Moreno with blood running down his face, crawl out of his sinking submarine during a hurricane, load the deck gun and fire one last shell into the German sub just before he drowned. That's guts. Art Acord is a chicken fake.

When I got home, I told mom about the knife. I asked her why they were so dumb to think we wouldn't catch it. Mom said, "Moving pictures are a brand new art. Painting was begun millions of years ago. Theater, music, sculpture and literature have been going on for thousands of years and they were done by artists. Now suddenly in the last few years or so we have motion pictures that are really an invention of technicians, not artists. So it's going to take some time before quality movies take the place of a train wreck, a punch in the jaw or a bullet in the chest...and come to think of it,maybe nevr. Then she laughed and laughed.

Jan 15 Saturday

Sun came out. Tom took our scout troop 16 on a hike to Camel's Back. Fish and I passed our cooking merit badge. We made a fire over some rocks and when they were hot we bent a piece of old wire screen over the rocks like an arch and packed wet mud over it to make a little oven. Then we laid our meat loaf on the rocks and covered the opening with more mud. Then we put some rice in a pan of water with a handful of raisins and hung it over a fire to cook.

The rest of our troop and troop 12 from the other side of town started playing Capture the Flag. That is a game that more guys get hurt playing one game than guys get hurt playing a whole winter of hockey. I think it's because the rules are never the same. The two teams each hide a flag within a certain area known to the opposing team. Then each team tries to get the other team's flag by force and carry it back to their own flag. You can tackle, trip, hide, throw mud (not rocks) make snares or deadfalls, pile several guys on one, etc. Also if two or three guys can capture one of the enemy and hold him in their camp they can use him as a hostage to get one of their guys who has been captured. Everything goes but no slugging. It's more fun at night, but then guys get twigs rammed in their eyes and one guy fell off Swallow's Cliff last year and punctured his spleen. He's still alive though.

Fish and I took turns guarding our oven but we both should have stayed on duty because all of a sudden I see this guy running right at our oven with two other guys chasing him. I threw a body block at the first guy and knocked him off line but one of the other guys stepped right on the oven and smashed it flat. Tom said to leave it alone and let it finish cooking. You can have a big hamburger instead of meatloaf and he laughed and laughed. Nothing ever bothers him.

At chow time we opened the oven. The meatloaf was flat as a pancake with an inch crust of dirt on the top. The rice pudding turned into glue, because, I guess, the water never got hot enough to cook the rice. Tom said, "If you eat three tablespoons of the pudding and some of the meatloaf you pass." We peeled the dirt crust back and ate most of the meat. It tasted pretty good. The rice pudding was tough to get down. It looked like glue. It hung from the spoon like glue, and tasted like Castor Oil. After watching us gag a couple of times, Tom said, "OK, one tablespoon." Erk.. we finally each got down one spoonful. We offered some to Trixie, Fritz's little black spanial, but she just sniffed it and backed away barking at us.

Jan. 16 Sunday

We got to the church at 9 with our hammers and nails. Gooses dad had a car and so did Jim. They drove us to the depot and we looked over the planks. They wern't too bad, and after sorting them out we had enough for the two long sides of the rink. The ends we can get later. We nailed triangle supports on the planks from Winshield's design and hauled the finished planks down to the rink. We laid rocks on the back of the supports and banked snow against them. The boards are only a foot high but that's high enough to bounce the puck back into play instead of losing it in the snow banks. We were done by noon. Jim is sure some Sunday school teacher.

Jan 17 Monday

Mr. Renner, my science teacher, is nuts about magic tricks. We all brought an old deck of cards to class. We put each squared up pack into a vise between two boards flush with the edge of the pack and then planed both ends of the deck so one side of the pack was shorter than the other like so:

You spread the cards out like a fan and have someone select a card, look at it and replace it in the deck without showing you what it is. While the sucker is looking at the card he chose, turn the deck end for end, so when he replaces the card the wide side of the card will be at the narrow side of the deck.

Then shuffle the deck several times; hold it behind you and locate the wide edge of his card by feeling the edge of the deck. Pull it out and they will think you are a magician.

Jan. 21 Friday

Snowed all week. No hockey. Blizzardy & cold. The temperature didn't get above zero all week night or day. Had to ski to school. Everybody brought their lunch so we didn't have to go home for lunch at noon.

Jan. 22 Saturday

Cleared up today. Trees are all covered with icicles. Ed came home from college and we all drove over to play the Hanska town team. Their team is sort of a mixture of kids and young guys like ours. The 3rd period was almost over and it was 3 to 3. There is one shot in hockey you get to use maybe once a year... if you're lucky. I got to use it and made a goal and we won.

I got a breakaway and went down the ice with only their goalie between me and the cage. I pretended to get ready to shoot and then went on by the cage and started to circle it. Well, their goalie made the usual mistake. He figured I was going to go all the way around and hook a shot in from the other side, so he turned his back on me and swung over to the other side. I cut to a stop as soon as he turned his back on me and went back up the same side I went by him on. When he realized he'd been suckered he threw his stick over against the post to stop my shot, but he was a split second too late. I slammed the puck against his stick and the puck rebounded off his stick and ricocheted into the net.

An experienced goalie will never take his eyes off the puck. He will turn to follow you with his back toward the RINK to see what you are going to do. And if you pull a reverse he merely jams his skate against the post as you come around and his skate deflects the puck away from the front of the cage. Theoreticaly the outstretched stick was supposed to have done

49

the same thing, but with the stick at arm's length there isn't enough force to hold the stick in place, so the puck merely bangs the stick away from the post and rebounds into the cage. Pretty clever, huh?

Jan. 23 Sunday

Went to Sunday school. We talked a little about the boards on the rink. Then we told Jim about the hike to Camel's Back and the "Capture the Flag" game. He said, "You mean they still let you play that? I was on crutches for two weeks once on account of that stupid game. It is nothing but licensed mayhem!" We all laughed. JR said,"I wonder if Mrs. Younger ever played Capture the Flag?" Then we really laughed. Jim tried to keep sober but didn't succeed very well. He said, "Why do they call it Camel's Back?" Nobody knew. He said, "On account of the 2 big hills which resemble a camel's humps, you dummies!" We had never thought about it, I guess.

Then he asked us about the 12 scout laws and we listed them on the blackboard. Then he asked us if we could condense some of them into fewer words. We discussed that for quite a while and finally agreed that trustworthy, loyal, helpful, friendly, courteous and cheerful might come under the heading of Kindness, and possibly, clean, because if you smelled, that wouldn't be very kind to especially a girl. Then the class was over and it seemed like it barely got started. Jim said we'd discuss obedient, thrifty, brave and reverent next time.

Jan. 25 Tuesday

Nothing happened. Oh yes, it did. Old Mrs. Stuse's cat wouldn't come down out of her big elm tree on the front lawn. About 4 o'clock the firemen came out with the hook and ladder and Hooks Peuser climbed way up and finally got the cat and brought him down. Mrs. Stuse had them all in for tea and cookies and invited us kids in too. Then we all said goodbye and waved. When they drove away they ran over the cat and squashed it flat. We started to run after them but Mrs. Stuse said, "No, no, wait. It'll just make them unhappy. Rags was over 12 years old and he was going blind anyhow. Come on in and have some more cookies and help me bury him."

We had to use a pick to get through the frozen ground but finally got a hole deep enough. She wrapped Rags in an old dish towel and then we covered him up. Tac made a little cross out of two branches and we stuck that in at the head of the grave. Then we said goodbye. Things can sure happen quick.

Mom decided tonight at supper that we would learn one new word from the encyclopedia each suppertime. Tonight she opened the first volume and read, "Aardvark, a burrowing animal of Africa that eats ants and termites. Noun." Charlotte said, "I'll carry that tidbit to my grave." Mom sort of looked crushed. Dad said,"What's the next one?" Mom read, "Aaron, the first high priest of the Hebrews. Noun." We all sat there. I said, "I'll mention his name when I apply for my summer job." ... Then dad said, "Em, are these string beans Stokeley's or Del Monte?" Mom sort of sighed and went out in the kitchen to see.

51

Jan. 26 Wednesday

The Minnesota River that winds back and forth along the northeast side of town is an old river. Sometimes it winds so much back & forth that the back cuts into the forth and makes a straight chanel again leeving behind a curved little lake called an oxbow. There were two of these oxbows near the hiway bridge leading out of town on the way to Minneapolis. Years ago the county decided to use them as a dump for debris and sand from county excavashun projects. They not only filled in the oxbows but extended the fill out into the river for about 100 feet next to some big oaks growing along the bank.

Pete Stern built a shack on this land several years ago and lives there with his retarded son, Jay. Sometimes we guys bicycle down to visit with Pete. He is a lot of fun. He taught us how to make willow whistles by tapping the bark loose with the backs of our knives. He also flattened out a big area about twenty feet on a side so we could play marbles there. In town everything is mostly covered with asphalt, gravel or concrete. He makes furniture out of tree branches and sells some now and then for cash. He taught us how, and so we all made one and some of us made two, so there are about 18 chairs sitting out in front of his shack in the shade under the oaks. We kept telling him he ought to sell them, and make some money, and he said, "Then I wouldn't have the chairs you kids made. They're worth a million bucks right there." And he'd laugh uproariously. "What say I save them for a rainy day?"

The shack itself is made of everything: Wood boxes, old tires, galvanized corrugated roofing, tar paper, cardboard boxes for insulation and old horse blankets for the inside walls. He painted the outside all different colors he scrounged out of the dump from thrown away paint cans. It has sort of a fairy tale, Hansel & Gretel look. We guys all wish we had a place like that for our clubhouse.

Inside there is an old oil barrel for a stove. He keeps Jay and himself fed with bullheds he catches in the river, day old bread from Eibner's and Schroeder's bakeries, and some vegetables the grocery stores put out on a free table if they get too old to sell to normal people.

However, suddenly last month, there appeared a notice in the Legal Notices of The Brown County Journal that there would be a hearing regarding Peter Stern's property on Friday, January 28 at the County Courthouse at 4 o'clock. We asked Pete what it was all about, and he said some woman complained to the county about this "old hermit" in his unsightly shack corrupting the youth of the town and not paying any taxes.

Anyhow, today we had all biked down to see if we could help him out, because he's a nice guy and also he's the underdog against all the snobs in town. He laughed and said, "Well, one place is as good as another." And kept on whittling on a wooden unicorn.

About five o'clock who should drive up but JR's dad and two young lawyers from town. JR's dad is in real estate. They asked Pete if they could help out and Pete said maybe they could. So they started talking and all of a sudden the lawyers started to laugh and JR's dad slapped his knee and said, "No kidding!" We asked what was so funny and one of the lawyers, Heine Samson, said, "We can't divulge our case right now, but wait until Friday." Then they shook hands with Pete and Jay and left.

Jan. 27 Thursday

After school we were having a snowball fight in our
forts on the hospital grounds. We had all agreed not
to yell, so all you could hear was the splat of
snowballs and an occasional muffled grunt when
somebody got it. Then Heine Samson pulled up in
his Flint Roadster and motioned us to come over. So
we went over and he asked us if we would be
character witnesses for Mr. Stern at the hearing
tomorrow. Of course we all said yes. But Heine said
that we should each think of something nice to say
about Mr. Stern. And not make up anything, but just
tell the truth, if we were asked by either the judge
or the lawyer to speak. Boy, things are looking a lot
better for Pete now that Heine and JR's dad are on
his side. They are pretty smart and everybody in
town knows them.

Jan. 28 Friday

We kids all tore over to the Court House after school.
About half the town was there. Judge Matherson
rapped for order at four o'clock sharp and asked the
woman complaintant to state her case. Her lawyer
stood up and described Pete's place as dirty, smelly
and disreputable. He accused Pete of fishing in the
river without a license; keeping a retarded son that
should be in a public institution and squatting on
public land to avoid paying property taxes. He
concluded by saying Pete was corrupting the young
boys in town. That didn't sound too good. I couldn't
see much of a silver lining coming out of this one.

When he finished, the judge asked the defense to
tell their side. Heine got up and asked, "How many
people here have fished in the river without a
license?" Almost the entire courtroom raised their
arms and there was a lot of laughing and the judge
had to rap for order and then cautioned Heine that
because everybody broke the law in this case had

nothing to do with the case at hand and Heine ought to know better and refain from any more theatrics or else. Heine apoligized, but we kids knew he had made a point to the audience. Heine then produced a document dated last month from a county health inspector that Mr.Stern's property plus the outhouse was properly kept and posed no health hazard. Then Heine said, "I would like to call a few character witnesses." As he called us kids by name we each stood up and said something about how Pete had shown us how to build furniture, make willow whistles and given us a big place to play marbles, etc. After the last of us spoke we all clapped and whistled until the judge had to shush us up with his gravel. Heine then asked how many people here would think that Jay Stern would be better off than he was now in the state asylum at St. Peter? Only a few hands went up besides the woman's and her lawyer's.

"Rebuttal", said the judge.

Her lawyer said, "The fact still remains that he is a squatter on public land and is not paying taxes. Wouldn't that be nice if we all could have a deal like that. My client feels the law should be upheld and Mr. Stern and his son should be ordered to leave town."

"Defense?" said the judge.

This time JR's dad stood up and said, "You all know that I've been in real estate in this town for years, so I did some digging into old records. Yes, Mr. Stern does not pay taxes, but there is a legal reason for it. The land that Mr. Stern is living on was unclaimed land up to a year or so ago. When the county covered the oxbow lakes with fill it extended the fill about 200 feet past the river bank to protect the oak trees growing along the bank. This, according to law became new land and remained unclaimed. The county did not file a claim on it as it ordinarily must do, probably because of an oversight of such a small plot.

Pete.. Mr. Stern built his house on it several years ago and then last year realized he had not been sent a property tax bill. So he went to the county assesors office and discovered he had built on unclaimed land. The clerk told him that he could file for title, and that if he built a house on it and lived there a year, the title would be his for life, or until he sold it. Herewith is a copy of the title application form. The year will be up in June and then Mr. Stern will have to pay taxes like all the rest of us with titled land. Sorry about that, Pete."

The room broke into applause. Then judge Matherson said to the woman's lawyer. "Do you mean you initiated these proseedings without checking on whether Mr. Stern owned the property or not?" The lawyer stammerd out that he had assumed... but the judge cut him short with sort of a shake of his head and a snort, mumbling something about modern lawyers not being dry behind the ears. Then he said that the court costs would be sent to the lawyers office and that he could deal with his client as to how the costs would be shared. Case dismissed for lack of substanshiating proof.

He then called the woman and the lawyer up to his bench and warned the woman that after this she had better be informed before she went around accusing people of things she made up. And that she was lucky if Mr. Stern didn't sue her for defamashun of character. But Pete told us later outside, that he probably wouldn't win a case like that, becuz at his age he couldn't possibly get a more defamed character than he already had. Eh,eh. Anyhow the good guys won this round.

Jan. 29 Saturday

Nothing happened. I'm not going to write for a while.
I think I've got writers cramp from writing
yesterday. I'm never going to be a court reporter.
Maybe I'll write some more when the weather gets
warmer. Dad gave me two dollers for December and
January. I owe him 7 days or 23 cents, because
January isn't over yet.

* *

Mar. 25 Friday

Gess I'll start writing agen. Goose, Fish, Fritz and I
just set a record. There was a scout jamboree at the
armory tonight. One of the contests was fire by
friction. There are 4 scouts on each teem. On the
word Go, the first scout starts whipping his bow
back and forth on the spindle. As soon as he gets a
spark on his tinder he picks the tinder up, cups it in
his hands and blows on it or swings it around his hed
until it bursts into flame. Then the second scout can
start making his fire. The first teem to get fire from
the 4th scout wins.

There were 11 troops ther from diferent towns. We
not only finished first, but we did it in one minute
and 44 seconds. That's averaging 24 seconds apeece.
We beet the old record for the Minnesota Area Valley
Council by a whole minute. Tom congratulated us but
said,"That record will probably last for a hundred
years, becuz more and more peeple are using
lighters instead of those ridiculus contrapshuns." So
we jumped him and dragged him down on the floor
and made him say "Uncle" three times.

Tom had got us some special hard Yucca wood from
Mexico to use for our 6 sided spindles and the
bottom slab. For the top block we used the glass top
off a coffee percolater. For the tinder we pounded

dried caulking rope until it was almost powder, and it sure worked. The slightest spark would set it on fire. We used a rawhide leather boot lace for the bowstring with an ash branch for the bow, cuz the ash branch had more spring to it than other branches and would keep the bowstring taut around the spindle.

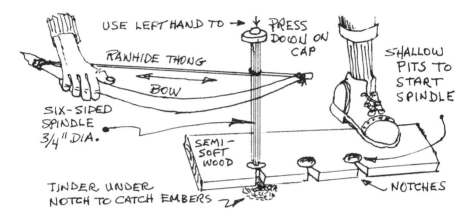

Goose was our best man. He got fire in about 8 seconds, which gave us a head start. He duzn't even look to see if he has a spark, he just whips his bow back and forth about ten times, grabs his tinder and POOF it bursts into flame. We guys don't know how he does it. Maybe he's part indian.

Mar. 26 Saturday

Loyd, Fish, Fritz Tac and Windshield and me hiked out to Redstone Quarry. The quarry is an old open pit with an opening on one side. There is an old ore-car track that winds down through the opening to a rotting loading dock about a hundred yards away next to a weed covered road.

Winshield was poking around in the dynamite shack and found a box of dynamite caps. They are little copper tubes with fulminate of mercury in one end.

The label on the box said not to carry them loose in your pocket. You stick the mercury end in the dynamite and poke the end of a powder fuse in the other end, light the fuse, and run.

We couldn't find any dynamite sticks or fuses, so we laid one on the ore track and dropped a rock on it. WHAM, it went off and YEOW did we all jump. It blew little pieces of copper into our ankles. That hurt. We didn't do that again.

Then we got a neat idea. We straightened the track out. Filled in the quarry holes here and there until we got the track fairly leveled. Ore rails are much smaller and closer together than regular train tracks. They are made to drag here and there to different places in the quarry so, so it was easy to lay it out where we wanted it. There were 3 old ore cars lying on their sides. We wrestled one upright, got it on the rails and put a slab of redstone under a wheel to hold it. The car was about 8 feet long with four-foot high steel sides front and back.

We laid the dynamite caps all along the rails, came back and climbed aboard. Three of us one one side , two on the other side and Loyd on the back. I kicked the slab out and away we rattled. The idea was to see who could stay on the longest. We hit the first caps.. Wham, wham, wham and then we began to pick up speed. More whams and the car started jumping and rocking around. We hit about twenty when we all bailed out about the same time except Loyd. Most guys can run about 17 miles per hour, and if you leave a moving vehicle much above that, you are going to be a rolling ball of bruises. But there went Loyd hanging on the back of the swaying car, careening along toward certain death. But then he lowered hinself down, put a foot on each rail and slid along on the track until about fifty feet from the end of the loading dock, when he let go and went sliding along by himself. The ore car sailed off the end of the dock, butt over teakettle through the air and smashed into the trees on the other side of the road, CRASH !, while Loyd finished his slide teetering on the ends of the rails on the dock. That was cutting it pretty close. I noticed he took a couple of big breaths before he turned and bowed and we all clapped. He won. He should be a stunt man like Yakima Canute.

Mar. 27 Sunday

We decided to build a tennis court, cuz the adults were always using the south-side park courts and the Haeberle's clay court. There is an empty lot between the Haeberle's court and the Walsh's house. We weeded it first and then leveled it with shovels. Took us all day.

Mar. 28 Monday

After school we tamped and stamped the dirt down until it was flat and hard. Then we tore up old sheets for the lines and held the strips down with square staples we made of coat hanger wire. Did you know there are over 500 feet of lines on a tennis court ? I know it now. We got the whole court laid out by 6:30 when our folks started yelling for us to come home.

Mar. 29 Tuesday

After school we dug 3 foot deep holes for the net posts, scrounged a couple of 8 foot pipes from the dump, put them in the holes with some rocks and tamped dirt. Karl Schmidt, who runs the camera shop is nuts about fishing and gave us a piece of old minnow seine for a net. It is only about two feet wide and 24 feet long but that is enough to hold any balls back. We sewed a clothesline into the top by folding the net over the rope and sewing it together.

Mar. 30 Wednesday

Played today for the first time. We don't have any
backstops so whoever isn't playing has to shag balls
behind the baseline. Mrs. Haeberle gave us some old
tennis balls. We only have 4 rackets. Three of them
are pretty good. They only hav a couple of strings
missing. The 4th one hardly had any strings at all, so
Fish swiped some strings from his brother's ukelele
case. We strung eight across and eight up and down,
pulled them tight and pounded match sticks into the
holes to hold them tight and used a double overhand
knot on the ends to keep them from sliding back
through the holes. They hold fine, but you have to hit
the ball in the exact middle of the strings or the ball
will go right through. Whatever side won a game had
to use that racket for the next game. That evened
things out. Mrs. Haeberle said that was ok, because it
taught us to hit the ball in the center of the head or
else.

Mar. 31 Thursday

Played more tennis after school and more after
supper. When it got dark we met with some kids
from Goose Town and Wallahi and started a game of
prisoner's base at the intersection of 6th and State.
We mixed up the players, because if we don't we
always get into fights about who's cheating who.

Our side had four prisoners for quite a while and the
two guys left on the other side couldn't get them
free. And we couldn't catch them. So the prisoners
started to get bored. Somebody suggested they start
throwing stones at the arc light hanging over the
intersection. So they did. Winshield and I told them
to stop. They said we were chicken. Winshield said,
Let's go, so we just left the game and walked back
down State to Windshield's house.

eld's dad is the City Clerk and Windshield what it costs the town because of vandals. We ____ out half way to Windshield's house when someone hit the bulb and there was a big flash of light. We looked back and one of the electric cables was burning on the end. Then it burned through and the end fell to the ground and sputtered out. Now it was pitch black and we could hear the guys all running away. The idiots had just smashed the only arc light within four blocks and screwed up our evening playground light for months. How stupid can you get?

When we got to his house his dad came out in front and asked us what the big flash was. We told him. The Windshield said, "They called us chickens and will be bugging us tomorrow with snotty remarks." His dad said to come in for a minute. So we went into their sunroom and sat down. His dad said, "Let me tell you something boys. Life is going to be that way for the rest of your lives. All you have between you and the bastards in life is your own character. You did what every citizen has to do, you stood up for right against the mob. Remember also that doing the right thing doesn't mean you'll be praised. Too often you'll be called a lot worse than chicken.

If they do sound off tomorrow, call them gutless criminals. You notice how they all ran away in the dark. Criminals live in the shadows. They prey on all of us. You may think I'm getting carried away here about a few kids plugging an arc light, but let me point out here that the city has to replace about 3 arc lights a month. Drunk adults shoot them out with 22's. Each light costs the city from $200 to $300 to replace, because it's not just the cost of replacing the bulb. Oftentimes the sockets are fused to the metal supports and pulley cables, so we have to get the hook and ladder out to cut it loose and replace the entire cable system plus the socket. Three arc lights per month equals nine hundred dollars. In one year this costs the city over ten thousand dollars, not to mention other vandalism.

The high school band room and gym get broken into. Criminals take band instruments and athletic equipment. Men break into the fairground sheds and swipe parts from the maintenance machinery. Others paint obscene words on our monuments, and so on. This is a town of 9000 population. If all vandalism stopped for just two years we could have a brand new public swimming pool with the savings. But the stupid criminals act like an octopus. Their tentacles reach out and touch every kid in this town. Mark my words. Some day a youngster is going to get killed out at that Cottonwood dam where you all swim between hidden rocks, rotting timbers and rusty spikes.

When it happens, every one of those kids throwing rocks at that arc light will be resposible for that youngster's death, just as surely as if they had shot him."

He stood up. "Well, that's quite a lecture, I guess. Your actions tonight may not affect the stature of America in the world scene right now. But, believe me, Billy and Winfield, it's kids such as you and the action you took that eventually affects the whole goddamn world!" And then he laughed. "And while you're affecting the world, let's go down to the Silver Latch and get a malt."
So we did.

Apr. 2 Saturday

Couldn't write yesterday cuz I got home too late. It was April Fool's Day and we pulled off a smasher. Herman's Monument is a statue of Herman the Great from Germany. It is on top of the hill by the Loretta Hospital. He stands on a dome held up by Greek columns forty feet high. He is 16 feet tall and holds a sword upright in his right hand above his head. He is made of iron. There is a circular staircase up the middle column leading to a room under the dome. The place is not kept up very well. There are weeds all around and the trap door opening into the attic is sort of rotten. Ther's a light on top of Herman's helmet you can see for miles around. Well anyhow, as soon as it was dark eight of us biked up center street and climbed up into the attic. We brought along 3 flashlights, a couple of rolls of red and white crepe paper, and an elctric fan we chipped in for and bought at the church rummage sale last month plus two extension cords. Loyd climbed out one of the little round windows in the dome and laid the fan on the cdgc of the dome facing upwards. We cut about ten strips of crepe paper and Loyd taped them to the fan grill. We plugged the extension cords into an outlet in the attic and Loyd started the fan going full blast blowing the crepe paper streamers upwards like mad. We handed the flashlights to Loyd and he set them around the fan so they shined upward on the streamers. It sure looked like a fire flame.

We got out of there fast and biked over behind the hospital and waited... and waited...and waited. Nothing happened. Guess nobody spends much time at night looking up at Herman. At nine o'clock we got tired of waiting, so we biked down Center Street hill and over to the Silver Latch. The cook, Booby Hatch, was standing outside the back of the cafe smoking his pipe. We asked him if we could use the phone. He said, Sure.

Now Loyd's older sister, Lil goes on night operator duty on the town switchboard at 8 o'clock at night., but we forgot that. We were going to call the fire station and tell them we thought we saw a fire on

Herman's Monument, but when Loyd picked up the phone and asked for the fire station's number, Lil said, "Is that you, Loyd?" He panicked and said, "No, it's not me." and hung up. Yikes, what a boner. We stood looking at each other sort of stupid like. Booby says, "What's the matter, boys? You the kids that set Herman's foot on fire?" I was about ready to start running when we heard the fire engine siren and then the hook and ladder came roaring around the corner and headed up Center Street hill.

Booby laughed and said, "I saw it a minute or so before you showed up when I first came out here and called it in." "Don't worry. We're well aware of April Fool's jokes here in the cafe. Sugar in the salt shakers, salt in the sugar bowls, rags in the pancakes and the juke box set to play only one record "Hymn of Ages", but a hot foot for Herman is at least original." He knocked the coals out of his pipe and said, "You know, if I were you, I'd split up and go home. Eight guys together on bicycles at 9:30 at night on April Fool's day
are a dead giveaway." We did. I got to thinking on the way home that maybe I was starting down the road toward being a criminal. Suppose one of the firemen got killed trying to get to that fire? Kids are stupid. I had a hard time going to sleep.

Now I'll write about Saturday.

Played tennis all morning. I felt better at lunch because dad told me that Hermans hotfoot was all over town and I guess nobody got killed or he would have said something. Come on, Stupid, THINK after this before you pull off a dumb trick like that!

Started to rain about noon and then the sun came out but the court was full of puddles. That showed us where the low spots were, so
we quik filled them with dirt and tamped it down. It's real level now.

We all went over to Gooses and got a lot of old corn cobs and chicken fethers. You stick the fethers in the end of the cob to make them fly straight and then you can throw them at each other. Bunny & Babes dad is a salesman and he has a lot of big empty carboard boxes in their garage. We made shields with arm bands and hand holds. We each start with 5 cobs stuck in our belts. If you stop a cob with your shield you can keep it. But if you get hit on the body or leg or arm you have to give the guy that plugged you all your cobs except one. At the end of the game the guy with the most cobs wins.

We played until about 3 o'clock. Then the fethers got so beat up the cobs wouldn't fly straight any more. So we went down to Schlumpburgers Meat Market to see if they had any extra feathers left over from chickens or turkey slaughtering. Mr. Schlumpburger told us to go around in back in the allcy where they do the slaughtering and ask Poik Schuman. They do the slaughtering in the meat market basement, and they usually open the doors onto the concrete apron in the alley so it doesn't get too smelly inside.

When we got there Poik was wrestling a pig around and tying the back feet together with a rope. The pig was squealing and lunging around but Poik finally got the feet tied and slung the end of the loop over a block and tackle and hoisted the pig upside down about a foot off the concrete. You never heard such squealing and snorting in your life. Then Poik hit the pig between the eyes with a small sledge. Crunch. That stopped the squealing and the pig hung there limp. Poik looked up and said, "Can I help you guys?" Between the stink from the hides and guts lying around, the squealing and the crunch, it took us a few seconds to remember what we had come for.

Goose was the first to come to and told him what we wanted. He went inside and came out with a gunny

sack half full of feathers and said, "Is this enough?"
Fish said, "Yes sir, I believe we can now outfit our
entire Indian tribe." Poik then did a couple steps
like an Indian dance, bobbing up and down and said,
"Me not give great spirit feathers to any Tom Tom,
Dick Dick or Harry Harry." That was a pretty fast
comeback. We all laughed and laughed. We asked him
if we could stay and watch, and he said,"Boys, I
wouldn't recommend it." We said, "Aw, come on,
Poik." until he said,"Well, ok, on one condition. When
you feel your mouth start to water get out of here
fast, because that's a sure sign you are about to lose
your lunch. And I don't relish, excuse the word,
having to clean up after people. The animals are
sufficient thereof unto the job at hand."

I said ok with the others, but already I was having
trouble swallowing with that stink hanging in the air
and that pig slowly rotating in the middle of the
arena.

He took a big hooked knife and slit the pigs belly
open from groin to throat. Tac and JR left. Then he
reached in and scooped out the intestines, liver and
kidneys and laid them on a sheet of butchers paper
on top of a pile of hides. Babe left. With a razor sharp
knife he skinned the carcass until the complete
skeleton was exposed. The teeth were grinning at
us and the two eyes looked like white billiard balls
staring at you. Bunny and Windshield raced to the
end of the alley. Bunny won and heaved into the
gutter. When Winshield saw him, he let go too.
Winshield always had a sensitive stomach since he
smoked that creosote cigarette. Poik watched them
go and said,"Yah, people always want their steaks and
bacon, but they certainly don't want to know where
they came from." He wore rubber boots. He hosed
down the carcass before he lifted it on to a big
butcher block table where he proceeded to saw and
chop up the steaks and roasts. I asked him whether

it bothered him to hit the pig, and he said only if he had eye contact with the pig, so he never looked the pig in the eye beforehand. He said he was a vegetarian.

When he started removing the brain from the skull I felt my mouth start to water and I gagged. Fish looked at me and we both started running down the alley to fresh air. Goose was the only one who stayed to the end. We waited for him and when he came out he had the bag of feathers and a printed card that said:

This is to certify that the bearer of this card had the intestinal fortitude to witness an entire dissection and is now a member of The Odor Of Butchers.

Signed: *Armand Schuman*,

That smell was really something. There were only three people in town that could stay in that alley during butchering days. Mr. Schlumpburger, Poik, and Paul Scheffer, who lost his nose in the World War somewhere near Amiens, France. Mrs. O'Malley, who lived 4 blocks away in Goosetown, complained in the Journal's "You Said It" column for subscribers, that the smell was killing her Begonias. In fact, I always doubted that story about Winston Churchill escaping from the enemy's prison during the Boer War by hiding under a stack of hides on a train. Because if he'd really laid there for 3 days, like my history book says, he would be blind.

Apr. 3 Sunday

Jim Becher is still our teacher. We never know
exactly what his opinion is. He asks us questions and
starts us arguing about the answer. We finished with
Thrifty, Obedient and Reverent, ok. Last week he
asked us to write down in the fewest possible words
what we thought our own personal philosophy on
religion was without telling anybody what it was. He
collected the papers today and listed the 8 religions
on the blackbord without our names so nobody knew
whose was whose. They were:

1. Be nice to everybody
2. Treat other people as if they were you.
3. Do good to people and pray for others.
4. When you see people in trouble help them.
5. Make a lot of money and use it to help others.
6. Be kind and help fight agenst crimnals.
7. Be trustworthy and teach others to be the same.
8. Don't hurt anybody unless they are doing bad
things.

Then Jim asked us what they all had in common.
After a while we decided that kindness was in every
one, just like our scout laws. And numbers 4,6 & 8
had an added idea of fighting against injustice. Then
he told us to see if we could lump them all together
and come up with one sentence. After a couple of
arguments we figgured that as far as we guys were
concerned, we could say that our religion was:

Be kind and work for justice for everybody when you
can.

Jim said next Sunday to bring a list of symbols that
people use in their religions. We could bring
examples of any religion and any country, and let our
folks help if we wanted to.

At Sunday dinner we had a pork roast, wouldn't you know. I kept seeing that pig dangling from the ceiling right over dad's head, while he was carving.

After dinner we all got together at South Side Park to play some baseball. I've got a catcher's mask and the catcher puts a couple of Saturday Evening Posts over each shin and holds them in place with innertube rubbers. George Glaser is our pitcher cuz he can throw pretty good. He's two years older than we are, but when we guys pitch it takes all day to make somebody out. After five walks the guys in the outfield are lying down, the shortstop stops jumping up and down and the third baseman is sitting on third base.

Some Goosetown kids came up and we got a good game going. George pitched for both sides. The score got to 18 to 21 and we decided to quit. We all started home on our bikes, when one of the Goosetown kids, Cliff, grabbed the back of Jinx Jacksons bike just as he started out to tease him. But he made a mistake. He did it the 6th time, which was once too often. Jinx threw down his bike and chased Cliff across the park, around the tennis courts, over the edge of the gravel pit and then after they slid down the loose gravel in the pit they climbed back up the rocks between the pits, ran across the park, around the courts and back down the pit again. When Cliff reached the top of the rocks the 4th time around he was so pooped he could only stagger for about 20 feet and collapsed on one knee, gasping for air. Right after him came Jinx crawling up over the last rock and when he saw Cliff he laid on top of the rock gasping for breath the same way. They looked at each other for about two minutes while the rest of us stood watching. Jinx did just not have the poop to go that last twenty feet. They kept looking at each other heaving away, and all of a sudden Jinx rolled over on his back and started to laugh. He just guffawed between gasps. Then Cliff started to laugh. Then we all started to laugh. I don't think any of us had ever seen anybody so exhausted they couldn't move another step. Anyhow, Cliff finally got up and told Jinx he was sorry and he shouldn't have done it and Jinx said, ok and they shook hands. All's well that ends well.

Apr. 4 Monday

Boy, dad brought me home a whole case of book matches from the Grocery Company. He says they are culls, left overs from production runs. The match company cases up these odd lots and sells them at a cheap price. Dad buys them and sells them to bars for a higher price than regular, because bar customers like to collect these different kinds.

I spent all last week sorting them out. They are from everywhere in the world. Wow! I have one from Rene's Pleasure Palace in Lima, Peru, with an Inca head on it. One from Toni's Beauty Parlor on Tan Jan Pandong Rd. in Singapore and a real ritzy one from Le Bal de Anglais at 6 Rue de Cannes, Paris, France. I have 2421 now. Dad says he buys 15 cases a month of these culls, and he'll bring me another case of 2400 next month, but I told him not to bother. I figured out that 2400 in a case means that the Grocery Company has a revolving collection of 35,000 different book matches each month. In a year I would have half a million book matches.

I have learned something about collecting. It doesn't pay to collect anything now a days unless it's rare like a toilet seat from King Tut's Tomb.

Apr. 5 Tuesday

Last week Mr.Renner asked us to bring him a single block of wood that would fit snugly into these four different holes.

Nobody could . So he showed us a piece of broomstick he had sawed off. The length was equal to the diameter of the handle and the sides were cut to a sharp taper like this.

Then he asked us to design a windmill that didn't turn into the wind but would run regardless of the direction of the wind. He can sure make us think. Even after school we keep talking about his problems and see if we can get the answer before the next day. He's like Jim Becher. He'll never tell you the answer. However, he will answer 4 questions per day for each student if it's toward the solution of the problem, with a yes or no. So you have to think out your questions pretty carefully to get the most out of his yes or no.

It's fun to be in his class. He never tells you you're wrong all the time. He pats you on the head and says,"Good going. You've almost got it." or something like that.

Apr. 7 Thursday

After school we all went over to Turner Hall gym to fence. There aren't any classes there Thursday afternoon and Tom lets us fence all over the place. Up and down the stairs, in the hallways and even hanging on the rings like Scaramouche. We all wear masks with throat aprons and the foils have buttons on the tips so we don't skewer anybody. There are two different schools, sort of. The French method is dextrous, quick and adroit, says Tom, whereas the Italian method is brutal, coarse and savage. Tom likes to fight the Italian way. Between flurries, he'll slam the floor with his foil and if you try to come in on him, he'll yell like an Apache and flip his foil up so hard it almost knocks it out of your hand. He lets three of us fight him at one time, like D'Artagnan, and we have never been able to touch him

He was some kind of champion fencer in Indiana when he went to college there. Dad told me that since Tom came to town we have had three captains of the University of Minnesota gym team in the last ten years, Stanley Simons, Ted Fritche and Leonrd Marti, Loyd's brother. Tom gave us kids "The Three Guardsman" by Dumas to read after we got interested in fencing and "Scaramouche" too. Those were some books. They sure beat the tar out of "Silas Marner" and "The Return of the Native" that we read in school. I'll bct Silas and the Reddleman never had a good laugh in their entire lives.

Anyhow, all eight of us were fencing and yelling in the gym Italian style when a Remington Typewriter salesman came in and tried to sell Tom a new model noiseless Remington. When he told Tom about the noiseless part, Tom shouted above the din below, "Why would I want a noiseless typewriter?" and the salesman left.

Later Tom asked us if we wanted to help out back stage Friday night for a road show that was coming in for a two night stand. We all said yes.

Apr. 8 Friday

After my Twelfth Street Rag lesson, I ran up to Turner Hall where the rest of the gang was and helped set up the scenery for the play. Al Fredricks was setting up the switchboard. Al owns a bar at the corner of Broadway and second north. He's one of the volunteer electricians for Turner Hall and is the best chess player in town. Judge Gislason is next. Al drinks a lot and has a habit of going into sort of a trance every now and then. It drives the judge crazy when Al sits motionless for severl minutes at the chess board, then raises his head and says, "Who's move is it?"

The curtain went up at eight o'clock. There was a full house. Both the dress circle and the balcony were full. It was a very dramatic play. The director played the part of the monk. He told Al he wanted the curtain to come down very slowly on the final scene. Al said, "Shure. Nushin to it." Well, the final scene came. The young couple embraced, were blessed by the monk and wended their way slowly upstage arm in arm into the forest as twilight descended on the monk standing there with bowed head. No curtain. The monk turns slowly and looks toward the switchboard. Al is in one of his trances. The monk coughs. Al jerks alert and hits the Fast Down switch. Down comes the curtain with a roar and hits the apron, kapow ! The monk rips off his wig, winds up and throws it at Al yelling, "I told you slow curtain, you stupid drunken idiot!" But when Al sees him tearing off his wig he brings the curtain back up fast and starts it down real slow. So the audience sees the monk throwing his wig across the stage and hears the last four words very clearly.

The director now senses the curtain is up and turns to see the entire audience laughing their heads off. What can he do but bow? When the asbestos finally got down there was a lot of cussing and stamping on the floor. If our moms would have been there, they would have covered their ears.

Apr. 9 Saturday

Spot and I were playing on the dirt court about 1
o'clock when a couple of ladies who were waiting for
the clay court to clear asked us if they could play
with us. We said sure, so they came over. We won 6
to 0. They were sort of surprised. Spot is a guy that
lives farther up State street and runs around with us
once in a while. He is a year older and just got his
driver's license. Once in a while he gets the family
Studebaker and we ride around town. It has a second
air jet that you open when you want to go fast.

He got it this afternoon and we drove out toward
Sleepy Eye when who should whiz by us but one of
the Bianchi girls. She had a new Essex. The knob in
the middle of the steering wheel is the horn but also
controls the lights, the heater vents and the starter.
Anyhow, Spot opened the second air jet and we
caught up to her after a mile or so but we couldn't
pass her. If we got even with her and started pulling
ahead, then slowly she would pull up even with us. It
was funny. We figgered out that it probably was
because the car ahead was forcing the air aside for
the car in back. I got an idea. I said close the
windows. We did and sure enough it streamlined the
Stude just enough so we could slowly pull ahead of
her. We were doing 75 and she was probably doing
74 and a half, because it took us about two minutes
to finally get far enough ahead so we could turn over
in front of her. But she turned off at Essig, the
Railroad Water Tank stop, and turned back toward
town. It was lucky we didn't meet another car
coming, cuz we did most of the racing on the wrong
side of the road.

Apr. 10 Sunday

We brought in our lists of symbols related to
religions and Jim put them up on the blackboard. We

divided them into Symbolic Things and Symbolic Activities. Here they are:

SYMBOLS	SYMBOLIC ACTIVITIES
Churches	Going to Church
Banners	Saluting a Flag
Chalices	Crossing ones self
Stained Glass	Taking communion
Scrolls	Reading the Scriptures
Bibles	Giving up meat on Fri.
Korans	No cloven hoof meat
Torahs	Bowing toward Mecca
Crucifixes	Traveling to Jerusalem
Six Point Star	Swinging a prayer wheel
Crescents	Reciting the Catechism
Icons	Lighting candles
Hammer & Sickle	Meditating
Idols	Fasting
	Chanting

Then we discussed why some people need symbols or symbolic activity to support their religious feelings. We didn't come to much of a conclusion except that some people felt they needed them and some people felt they didn't. When Jim asked us which items on the list were more important to us than kindness to others, it didn't take more than five minutes to come to an agreement. We said, "None." Then Jim said, "Ok, guys, I agree. but there are lots of people in the world that don't think the way you do. We'll discuss that next time."

Apr. 11 Monday

This week is test week in school because next week is Easter vacation. Nothing worth writing about. We've wasted all week on the "Legend of Sleepy Hollow". We've torn it apart 3 times for symbolism, and twice for figures of speech. That Ichabod Crane is probably the most moronic hero in English literature. I would put his IQ at about 54. Where do they get these stories that every guy in school thinks is stupid? Dad says I should remember that most teachers have been women over the years and they favor unrequited love and sentimental victorian dramas over blood and guts.

Apr. 15 Friday

Took my last test today. What a relief. Took my Rag lesson. I'm getting pretty good. I got the right hand down pat and I play the right hand while Miss. Christensen plays the left hand. It sounds great. Today I started on the left hand. I really practice hard at home now. Also I had to leave Dejah Thoris until the next book. She is in a round stone prison on the north pole of Mars with a retarded assasin. The prison revolves with the planet so the prison opening only comes around every Mars year. Mr. Carter and I will have to wait.

I was on my way home about 4 when I met Tac and JR. They were on the way to the meat market again. They wanted to try once more to see if they could get a card like Gooses. I decided to go along. When we got there Poik was killing about 30 chickens. I thought, thank God he isn't killing a cow. Poik said killing chickens was different. He said there was 3 ways to kill foul. You could chop the head off, wring the head off or snap the head off with the side of your hand. He didn't like snapping the head off, because the spinal cord would sometimes dangle down, which would give him twinge of nausea. But whereas the pig would hang there limp after the crunch, the chicken bodies would flop around for maybe ten minutes. Also the heads would lie there on the concrete and blink their eyes. There wasn't as much blood and guts as with the pig, but let me tell you watching 30 heads blinking away with their bodies flopping around ten feet away is something you don't see in your kitchen very often before a chicken dinner on Sunday.

Apr. 16 Saturday

We got up at 5:30 to play tennis. Mr. Walsh was not pleased. He called our folks at 5:40 and they were not pleased either. So we had to wait until 8 o'clock. Hal Soukup was home from St. John's College for Easter vacation and he was driving by when he stopped and watched us play. He got out of his car and came over. He plays number one at St. John's. He showed us a few things about grips, weight transfer forward, blocking a volley and some tactics. He stayed all morning giving us pointers while we played. When he demonstrated he sure looked smooth. Boy!

Apr. 17 Sunday

No Sunday school. There was a special Easter Service. We guys all had to go regardless of how kind we had been all week. Afterwards we fought Easter eggs. You hold the egg in your hand and smack it against someone elses egg. Whoever's egg cracks loses. The long narrow eggs are the best cuz the sharp point is a cinch to crunch the fat round eggs. I went home with five squashed dirty eggs. I would have had 6 but I gave one to Georgy Swartz. He wanted to throw one at Woodrow Baxter.

Spot got the Stude tonight. We decided to go hunting rabbits out on the fairgrounds. Two of us hang on the running boards on each side of the Stude, while Spot turned on the high beam headlights and we went racing over the grass until we flushed out a rabbit. Rabbits always run in a straight line ahead in the lights because that is the only place they can see where they're going. Spot would then gun it, and when we got close the two guys on the running boards would jump off running while the rest of us would pile out and finally corner it. Of course we would let it go then, but tonight Tac dived at the rabbit and accidently landed on it with his knee when the rabbit tried to dodge under him. There it lay, quivering. Nobody knew what to do, so I said, "I better kill it, stand back." I picked up the rabbit by the hind legs and brought my hand down on the back of its neck, just like Poik did. Sure enough, it went limp. Well, what I didn't realize was that when I hit the neck the head snapped back, the blood flew out of the rabbit's nose and spattered dots of blood across my face. In the dark nobody noticed. We all felt kind of bad that we killed it, so we quit and went home. When I walked into the living room, mom said, "My God. What happened?"

Well, I had to tell them the story and she said she had better tell Spot's mother before somebody got run over.

Apr. 18   Monday

I guess Spot's mother told Tac's mother and that ended the fairground chases, because Tac's uncle, Pete Aufderheidi, is the County Fair Chairman and he told the Brown County Journal today in the "You Said It" column that they were going to padlock all the gates so those vandals couldn't rip up the football field and dirt race track anymore. Spot said he couldn't drive the Stude for a month. Now we are all vandals. I'm afraid Windshield's dad will hear about me.

We figured out that if Mr. Walsh couldn't hear us playing in the early morning, he wouldn't care, so we pitched our pup tents between the alley and the court so we could get up at dawn without waking our folks.

Mosquitoes got us up about 4 am. It was still dark so we tried to play with flashlights. A guy stood by each net post with a flash and they'd follow the ball in flight. We could see the ball alright but we couldn't see our partner so we kept bumping into each other. The sun came up anyhow and we played in complete silence. If anyone shouted or called the score out loud he had to give up his racket to someone shagging balls.

In the early morning mist it felt like we were playing in a dream world. The rains, the mists and the damp court had gradually caused our rackets to get fuzzier and fuzzier. The one with Fish's Ukelele strings looked like an African Fly Whisk. When we hit the ball it sounded like swoosh instead of whack, which was ok because it cut down on the noise. Between the arguments about who was making noise and swatting at mosquitoes during a stroke we decided to call it quits about 6 and went home for breakfast. We all came back at eight and played all day. Mosquitoes don't like sunshine.

Apr. 22 Friday

Played tennis all day Wed.,Thu., and today. Jerry said I could use his racket, if I didn't let anybody else use it. It's a Dreadnought Driver. It has a steel frame around the head and twisted steel cables for strings. Jerry says it's 30 years ahead of its time. I haven't lost a game all week.

This evening dad answered the phone and I heard him say that no this wasn't the Jiffy Auto Parts store. And then he hung up. A few minutes later he got another call and then three in a row. Each time he'd just get settled in his arm chair and he'd have to lurch up out of it and get the phone. Mom yelled from the kitchen that the new Jiffy Auto Parts was having an opening this evening and was giving away free popcorn and NEHI pop. They probably got a number similar to ours, so just take the phone off the hook.

But no. Dad dragged his chair over to the phone and got that sneaky look on his face. The phone rings and dad says, "Jiffy Auto Parts at your service. Yes, we carry oil filters. What model do you want? Yes, we have that in stock. It's three dollars. You say you can get it at your garage for a dollar twenty? What is the address of your garage? Why? I'd like to buy a hundred or so. Hello, hello... wonder why she hung up?"

Then mom said, "Herman, you can't do that. You'll go to jail." and then she took the phone off the hook. He drives mom crazy.

Mom tells about when they first went together he had told her his first name was Wolfgang. She didn't find out his real name, Herman, for about two months, when a friend called him Herman while introducing them to a friend. Dad sheepishly admitted his name was Herman, but told her, "Who wants to date a guy named Herman?" Dad is pretty smart.

Once he cut holes in the front part of his black socks when they went to a party. During the party he worked the conversation around about how women are so busy nowadays they don't have time to do the housework or mend socks or anything. After the women all got arguing back, he said, "I can prove it!" Then he takes off his shoe and wiggles his toes through the holes right in front of all their friends. Of course the men all roared. Even mom had to laugh cuz it was so ridiculous. He is sure funny.

Mom told me another one when dad was trying to wall paper the ceiling in the sun room one afternoon, a kid came to the front door selling magazine subscriptions so he could go to college. Dad made him a deal that if the kid helped him wallpaper, dad would buy some subscriptions. Well, dad kept the kid for about 3 hours until the job was done and sort of felt obligated.

Mom said that's why we have all those magazines: True Detective, Black Mask, Wierd Tales, Crimes of Horror and that two-pound "Atlas of Animal Anatomy" by W Allenberger, et al, he got as a bonus. We use it as a doorstop on the back screen door.

When mom entertains her church circle she scurries around hiding all dad's magazines. I guess most of the ladies don't believe there is such a thing as crime.

Woody Gebhardt runs a construction company and is building a house on the empty lot next to the Puhlman's house on 7th North & State. He has a black Dachshund named Teddy. Teddy is always on the construction site with Woody. Anyhow the Puhlmans were going away for a few days and asked Woody if he'd take care of their goldfish and rabbit while they were gone. Woody said ok.

But no sooner did Woody get on the job the next day when Teddy came up to Woody with the dead rabbit in his mouth. Woody brushed off the rabbit; went over to the Puhlmans back yard, laid the rabbit in the hutch and closed the door. figuring they'd think the rabbit died in the hutch.

The Puhlmans came home on Thursday afternoon. Ten minutes later their 7 year old son, Jimmy, came running over to Woody and said, "Mr. Gebhardt, the funniest thing happened to Hippity Hop. The morning we left we found him dead in the hutch. It was early and you hadn't started work yet. Dad buried him by the back fence. Now he's back in the hutch. Did you know that?"

The only reason I know about it is that Woody told dad about it and swore dad to secrecy. But dad thought it was so funny he told Charlotte, me and mom and swore us to secrecy. Nobody important will ever read my diary, anyhow, so I figure Woody is safe.

Apr. 23 Saturday

A carnival is out at the fairgrounds. It unloaded this morning at the depot at 3 am. We all biked out to the fairgrounds about 6 and the ground boss said he'd give us each a ticket to the main show matinee if we'd help haul on the ropes, unload the crates,etc. It got pretty hot about 9 o'clock. There was a barrel of drinking water with some dippers hanging on the edge. During a lull I went over for a drink. I took a dipperful and leaned over the barrel so I wouldn't spill any outside the barrel. One of the roustabouts yelled at me, "Hey kid, get back from the barrel! You think we want your slobber in our drinking water?" I sure felt awful.

But a little later I was unrolling a canvas tarp with two of the roustabouts when Gretchen, Kathy and some of the girls walked by. Gretchen said, "I didn't know you worked with carnivals." and gave me a neat smile. Me being with those two big guys on the same job made me look real tough. There's always a silver lining. The carnival was opening at one. We finished about noon, got our tickets, biked home, had lunch and got back about 1:30.

We walked along the side shows first with about a hundred other people. In front of the tents were big paintings on canvas about 15 feet square. One was of a bearded lady. There was the fat lady too. A big guy with fangs was wrestling a boa constrictor. There was an Armadillo with a women's head and a naked Abysinian native with two pointed heads.

The next tent was Jojo, the dog faced boy. The painting showed a man's body with a dog head. The hawker was giving out a steady line of chatter."Ladies and Gentlemen, on the inside see Jojo the dog boy captured only months ago in Abyssinia. Born with fangs, paws for hands and double eyebrows to shade his eyes from the scorching African sun. You can now see him close up, howling and growling in the bottom of a pit with no danger to you." Then he told about paddling leaky dugouts down the headwaters of the Nile River pushing crocidiles out of the way with their bare feet."For just one dime you can have the thrill of seeing him eat a live chicken every hour." We went in.

There was Jojo alright, crawling around in a big canvas lined pit, growling and occasionally howling, just like the man said. There were a lot of bones and feathers lying on the bottom of the pit. He sure was well fed. He had real bushy eyebrows that hung over his eyes like a poodle. His hands were like furry paws with long cat nails sticking out, and he had two long fangs too, sticking out over his chin. He wasn't something you'd want for a pet.

There was a trainer standing beside the pit with a long stick to keep Jojo from crawling up over the edge and attacking the customers. If he did try to get us the trainer would beat him back. In between attacks, the trainer would beat the side of the canvas with his stick, Whap!. When he did Jojo would cringe and scramble over to the side of the pit and cower in the corner. The trainer said it was his scientific opinion that Jojo was the result of Abyssinian natives getting lost in the jungle and mingling with wild dogs and there was no hope of ever educating him. Then he threw him a dead chicken. We could tell it was dead because it didn't flop around like Poik's chickens did. Jojo snatched it up and bit some chunks of feathers off the chicken, took it over to a corner and bent over it with his back to the audience. The trainer then said, "That's it folks. Jojo doesn't like people see him finish off the chicken." So we filed out. I was the last one out. When I looked back, Jojo was standing up talking with the trainer while the trainer was lighting Jojo's cigarette. Jojo might not be very smart, but he sure learned English in a hurry.

The next tent was Charles, the ossified boy. The painting showed a real thin guy that looked as if he were painted with stucco cement. The man outside in front was making a pitch: "On the inside see one of the strangest medical marvels of modern times, Charles, the Ossified Boy. He is slowly turning to stone, but medical science has kept him alive for over 24 years." Then a nurse in a white uniform came out and described the disease in detail. Nobody felt much like shaking hands with Charles like the nurse suggested, so we started on when somebody said, "What a con game." But Fish said, "Not really. After all he's out making his own living. He's not sitting in a poorhouse, and we ought to be kind to him like Jim says." We said ok, but how? Fish said well, we could all buy a ticket and then tell him what a gutsy guy we think he is. So we all went in. Charles looked pretty awful. His skin looked like rough hard parchment. He couldn't move his joints and he could barely smile. But we all shook his hand carefully and each one of us told him we thought he had more guts than anybody we ever knew. When we filed out the nurse came out with us. She and the guy out front told us that Charles probably wouldn't live much longer and what we kids did was the nicest thing he would ever remember. Then she started to cry. Boy, you never know what's behind people's masks. And you know, if it hadn't been for Jim, we wouldn't have even thought we could have helped.

April 24 Sunday

Sunday school. Jim asked us if we'd like to help somebody out this afternoon. Of course, we all said yes. We'd go with Jim anywhere. He said a tree had fallen on Henriette Gorsham's front porch about a month ago and it was still there. We could probably fix it for her. Then we gabbed mostly about track records the rest of the time. Jim asked if we knew the fastest time in the 100 and we all said 9.4 seconds cuz that is the world's record. And he said would you believe I have run the hundred in 9.2? And we all said, "Oh Yeah?" Then he got up, sidled over to the door and said, "Well, it was with a running start. Class is over." and tore out of the door with us all chasing him. He is nuts.

We got to Henriettas about 1 o'clock. Jim brought two 12-foot 2x4's, a couple of saws and an axe. Henrietta came out and Jim introduced all eight of us. We said hello. We felt sort of foolish after throwing snowballs on her roof.

We started cutting all the branches off and stacking them up. Henrietta worked right along side of us. She is strong. Then we dug around the roots until they were free. We made an X out of the two 2x4's by lashing them together at the crossing. We stuck the X under the trunk close to the porch roof, and pulled. The X kept the tree from scraping the shingles of the roof. When it was free of the roof the whole thing fell over to one side, Crash. We sawed for a couple of hours until it was all sawed up into 18 inch lengths and stacked it on her wood pile. Then we raked and cleaned her whole yard and got ready to leave, when she went inside the porch and came out with her box of rocks. She went over and dumped them in a garbage can. Then she came over and shook each of our hands, one after the other and went back into the house without saying a word.

Jim said, "What was that all about?" I said, "She just left us flatfooted in the dust of human kindness." "Yeah," Said Fish," Symbolically speaking, she just did the hundred in 9 flat."

Apr. 29 Friday

The high school had a track meet out at the fairgrounds after school. They run the races on the dirt race track. Once around is a half mile. Goose and me hitched a ride out on a Dannheim Dairy truck. Donald Dannheim is in high school and drives for his dad sometimes. Today he was taking some drinks out to the food stand, so he picked us up. He plays tackle on the football team. One time he led a pep rally in the assembly before a game and didn't think the students were yelling loud enough, so he yelled, "Get the lead out!" right in front of the teachers. He is not snooty and picks us kids up every once in a while.

Anyhow he let us out and as we walked across the field toward the track Goose picked up an old tennis ball and we tossed it back and forth. When Goose tossed it to me this time it had a flap on it and I thought a piece of the cover had come loose. I reached up with my hand to flip it back at him, but it came right through my hand and hit me in the nose. I saw a big flash of light.

When I came to I was bouncing around in the back of Dannheim's truck with Goose squatting beside me. Donald stopped the truck at old Doc Hammermeister's house. Doc is retired but still keeps a small office at his house for emergencies. He is only a few blocks from the fairgrounds and helps out with emergencies from the race track and ball games there. Donald and Goose helped me into his office. I was a bloody mess and kind of woozy. Doc cleaned the worst off me with a damp towel and sat me down in a metal chair with a head rest. He looked into my eyes first with a little flashlight. Then he looked up my nose. He said, "Well, you are going to live, but I'd advise you to stay clear of that fairgrounds. That place is worse than playing "Capture the Flag". I couldn't help but laugh and I said, "You too?" And he said, "Yup."

Then he got out a long tweezer and picked out a small piece of bone from up inside my nose. That didn't feel too good and I started to sweat like mad. He said you're turning pale. Put your head down between your knees. I did and pretty soon the room wasn't tipping upside down anymore.

He took two pieces of shiny white cardboard, smeared them with vaseline and pushed one up each nostril. That didn't hurt much. He said, "What day is this?" We said Friday. He said, "You go see Doc Howard on Monday and let him take a look at you. He'll probably pull the splints out then. In the meantime they'll keep the blood from sticking your nostrils together." Then he looked in my eyes again and said he didn't think I had a concussion, but he would call my mom this evening and tell her about watching for concussion symptoms.

When we started to leave, Doc asked Goose how it happened. Goose explained that we were tossing the tennis ball back & forth and it dropped in the grass.

When he bent over to pick it up he noticed this iron flagpole top lying in the grass with a threaded flang sticking out of it. "So I picked it up instead of the ball and tossed it at him for a joke. I forgot to tell him it was made of iron." Then Doc said, "That's like Moses forgetting to chisel the `not' in the 7th commandment." Whatever that meant.

I thanked Donald and Goose when they dropped me off. I went in the house, but nobody was home. I went in the kitchen and looked in the mirror. Boy, I looked great. My nose was flatter, like a boxers. I always had sort of a long thin sissy nose. Now I looked tough. Boy, what a miracle. There's always a silver lining. Mom didn't think so when she got home.

Apr. 30 Saturday

They are tarring State Street. They started at Center Street and do about 2 blocks a day. They got to 4th South yesterday and will lay the tar down from 4th South to 6th South Monday. They put a bunch of metal barrels full of tar along the curb between 4th and 6th. The tar in the barrels is hard, but when they use it they heat it up and use a big machine to spread it. Then they come by later with a steam roller with water running over the rollers and smooth it down.

Well, anyhow, if you stand on the top of the tar in one of the barrels in your bare feet you gradually sink into it. We thought up a contest. However could sink into the tar the deepest would win. We started at one o'clock. We all stood on top of a barrel. Nothing happens at first, but after about five minutes your feet start sinking in a little. At 1:30 I was up to my ankles. At two o'clock the tar was half way up our shins. At 2:30 most of the guys got bored and pulled out. It took me 10 minutes to pull out each foot. JR was reading a May copy of "Black Mask", so he wasn't bored. Last month in the "Jade Dragon" Don Everhard was trapped in a Tong basement. His girl Tanya was tied to a chair. The Chinese thugs gave him two choices: Shoot the girl to prove he wasn't a spy or die the death of a thousand cuts. JR was so interested in finding out the ending that he hardly noticed we were all pulling out. We all put our Keds back on and hung around until he reached the end about 3:15. He won. Sort of. The tar was over his knees. So how do you get out when you can't bend one leg? We laid the barrel and JR down on the boulevard grass and tried to pull him out but it was hopeless.

Winshield ran across the street to his house and told his dad, cuz his dad is City Clerk. His dad came over and said, "How in sam hill?" And just shook his head and said, "Don't go away, JR, I've got to figure this out." And he walked sort of slowly back to his house. About ten minutes later he came back and said, "I was lucky to catch Rick Rinehart at home. He's going to see if he can get two maintenance men. If so, they'll be out pretty soon. If not, JR, you'll be lying there until Monday. I suppose we could rig a tent over you."

But pretty soon a truck pulled up and two guys got out. They started a blow torch and heated up the outside of the metal drum until they were able to slide the barrel off the tar with all of us pulling and tugging. Now JR is still sticking out of one end of the chunk of tar. They stood him upright and sawed some slices of tar off the side until finally they were able to pry some of the tar away from his legs and get his legs free. We all clapped. One of the men said, "Next time you kids do this, please do it on a week day. We'd like to keep our Saturday afternoons free. Ok?" and laughed. When they pulled away we all stood at attention and saluted them.

After JR got his shoes on, we asked him what happened to Don Everhard. JR said, "He shot his girl friend. Who would want to die the death of a thousand cuts?" We said, "Yeah... and it took you two hours to find that out." He said, eh eh, well actually there was more to it than that.

"The Tong thugs hand Don a forty five with one bullet in it and cover him with a Thompson sub machine gun. Don takes aim at Tanya and yells "Deader than Hell!" and shoots her." "So?" we say. JR continues: ".. between her upper arm and chest. And Tanya knew right what to do. She screamed and slumped forward as if she was dead, with blood dripping through her white blouse into her lap. Don says to the thugs, "Satisfied?" The thugs thought he was ok and as they walked up to him Don grabbed the Tommy gun and held them at bay while he untied Tanya. Then they had a running gun battle through the subterranean passageways under San Francisco Chinatown until Don was able to trick the Tong Chief into falling into a pit of vipers. Then they recaptured the Jade Dragon and returned it to the good Chinese above ground.

Dad had been down at the grocery company and he got home just after we freed JR. He asked me if I'd like to go look at a new car Martinka's garage just got in. When we got there the manager, Gene, asked us if dad would like a demonstration. It was the new Auburn Cord Touring car. He said it was the first front wheel drive car ever made and it wouldn't skid or slide because the front wheels pulled the car along instead of pushing it.

Gene drove us out on the gravel road toward St. George where they had been grading the road. The workers had left a two-foot high gravel winrow down the center of the road. Gene gunned it until we were going 70. He said, "Watch this." and turned the car left over the winrow and then back to the right, making a series of S's back and forth. As we careened along the gravel made a noise as if it was ripping out the bottom of the car, and the sand was blowing into my eyes in the back seat. Suddenly the Cord went up on two wheels and almost flipped over. I closed my eyes and hung on to the robe rail with both hands. Dad was yelling, "Ok,ok. I'm convinced. I'm convinced. Slow down!"

Gene slowed down then and turned around. On the outskirts of town steam started coming out of the engine. We stopped. The radiator had holes in it and the water was running out the bottom. Gene said, "I guess I got carried away." as we clunked, clunked back to the garage.

On the way home I said, "Wow, that is sure some car!" Dad sort of grunted and mumbled something about how beautiful the trees and blue sky lookcd. Sometimes I don't understand him.

May 1 Sunday

Jim thanked us for taking down Henrietta's tree. Then he said he was going to give us a quick history lesson about people in the world that think their religion and symbolic rituals are more important than kindness.

The early religions usually started out with our same ideas of kindness and justice. But as they developed the leaders got more power and started yelling that their religion is the only way to salvation and would kill anybody that didn't think that way.

In India, for example, about 100 BC, the Brahmin priests set up the Hindu caste system, because they were afraid too many guys from the dark skinned races in southern India were getting into their priestly bureaus. That dumb prejudiced system lasted for 2000 years. Some religion.

He told us about the Italian and Spanish Inquisitions when church leaders had people tortured and killed if they didn't accept the church's teachings. Some religion.

During the 12th century the Christians in Europe sent army after army into the holy land to take it away from the Muslims. They even sent children. Thousands of these children and soldiers died more from disease and starvation along the way than did during the fighting.

In the 1500's AD, John Calvin had a Spanish priest burned at the stake cuz he wouldn't believe Calvin's religion. Mine is the only way to think, said this guy Calvin. We all agreed he must have been a real dope.

In the 18th century the Catholics drove many of the Protestant Huguenots out of France for the same kind of dumb reasons.

Now in the 20th century the Russians allow no religion at all. They took away all the churches and said that if the people didn't become Athiests and swear there was no such thing as God they would ship them off to Siberia to freeze to death. What a bunch of nincompoops.

We guys had never heard about these people before. We could hardly believe that whole countries were that stupid. We gabbed a while longer and finally agreed that when any religion says that if you don't believe like they do you are dead meat, they are stupid and mean or want to bilk you out of your money.

May 4 Wednesday

State street is tarred and rolled. After school we played polo on our bikes between 5th and 6th on State. We had 4 on a side. We each had a croquet mallet and used a croquet ball. But on the first hit it rolled past everybody, hit the curb and rolled down 5th street, past Broadway, across Minnesota street and all the way down to German street where it bounced over the curb into the brush. It took us 15 minutes to find it and we decided a croquet ball wasn't going to work. We went over to the Union Hospital addition and asked one of the construction guys if they'd give us a chunk of 4x4. He cut off a four inch section and then nicked the eight corners off. He said that would be better than just a square block cuz he had tried a croquet ball the same way 20 years ago. How about that. We thought we had invented bike polo.

We started again. This time the block would slide or tumble along and not go so fast. We played for about 20 minutes and then had to quit. There were only three bicycles still operating. Croquet mallets are hard on spokes.

Went to the church Wednesday night supper. I hate church suppers. All us kids have to eat in the basement. It has a real low ceiling, and it's hot because it is next to the kitchen where a lot of old ladies with rags tied around their heads carry pots around and sweat a lot. We get cold mashed potatoes with a teaspoon of white gravy in the middle and one glass of luke warm water. I can hardly get my mouth unstuck after two mouthfuls.

May 6 Friday

Senior skip day. Seniors at the high school skip the whole day. It isn't supposed to be legal, but nobody does anything about it and it's sort of a tradition. We guys think the seniors waste a lot of time driving by the high school and yelling all day when they could be swimming at the Cottonwood dam or wrestling. Anyway, Fish heard his older sister talking on the phone about having a weiner roast by the Cottonwood river near the old haunted house tonite.

After dark me and Fish biked out to the haunted house and stashed our bikes in the woods. It was bright moonlight. We knew that the guys would bring the girls to the haunted house so they'd scream and yell and pretend to be afraid. We were walking up to the back of the house when we heard voices. My god, they were coming to the house BEFORE the roast. Well, we ran like mad to the back of the house. There was a window up about ten feet with a pile of manure and dirt under it. Fish took a run up the pile, grabbed the sill, hauled himself up and squatted on the sill. I had run around the side of the house and there was a doorway. I stood in it and looked up at Fish. I said, "Here's a door." He said, "Oh well." and jumped down. He went right through the floor into the basement, Crash! I waited to hear him moving. Nothing. I whispered, "Are you ok?" He said, I think I've been blinded. I can't see a thing." I said, "Neither can I, Dummy. The moon just went under a cloud." Fish said, "Some cloud." Then. "I see the stairs. Get down here quick." I felt my way down the steps and we sat there waiting.

Pretty soon they came up on the front porch. The boys were groaning and hissing like ghosts, and the girls were giggling like idiots. We let them get inside and then we started howling and snarling like mad wolves. There was a sudden silence upstairs. Then everybody took off through the front door, over the porch, and down the hill. And I mean everybody, even the boys. Scardy cats. Fish and I went up and stood on the porch laughing like mad.

All of a sudden we could see some of the guys turn and start back up the hill. They probably realized they'd been fooled. We jumped off the porch and hid in a clump of bushes. As we watched the guys creeping up the hill they all seemed to be bent over before they reached the top. What Fish and I couldn't see was a single strand of barbed wire still left on an old fence that they were ducking under.

We waited until they were all inside. They had flashlights now. Then we made a mistake. We started howling and snarling again. They came tumbling out of the door on to the porch. Silence. Then we made another mistake. We shook the bushes and snarled again. They almost panicked, but caught themselves and came running at the bushes. We took off running along the the side of the hill. Fish was faster than me. He suddenly swerved and ran down the hill, probably figuring he could make more speed. He was right, but he ran full speed into that barbed wire fence. He did a complete flip and landed this time on his butt, thank god. I saw him fly but I couldn't stop so I tried to hurdle it. I got my left heel over the wire but couldn't pull my right leg over. A barb caught my leg, tore a chunk out and I did sort of a cartwheel to land beside him. We got up and ran another couple hundred yards when we hit the river bank, but we kept right on going and swam to the other side and laid in the mud amongst the cattails. The barbed wire fence had held them up or they would have caught us for sure. There's always a silver lining. They came to the river and stopped - thank the lord. We were pooped and gasping. They yelled at us that they knew who we were and were going to get us tomorrow. Ha, Ha, that's an old one. But then I thought about that girl baby sitter at the Kempski's and wasn't so sure they didn't know.

When we finally stood up and sloshed up the bank, Fish looked like a Fiji Islander. He was covered with mud. There was white cattail cotton all over his hair. And what was left of his knickers was hanging in strips from the bands below his knees. We were both bleeding from the barb cuts. That was sure a fun night.

May 7 Saturday

A Medicine Show came to town today. They set up
on south Broadway in a sloping meadow just where
the road takes off for the Cottonwood dam. They
have two closed trucks that open up on the back to
make a stage level with the truck beds. There were
two men and two ladies that did the acting and
another man that makes the pitch for the medicine
and also tells the plot from the side as the play goes
along.

The plays are short skits and pretty funny. Some of
the jokes are old ones, so the audience knows what's
coming, but the way the actors say them and make
asides to the audience like corny western movies, it
is really funny. There's always the hero, the heroine,
the villian and the good, bad girl. About fifty people
stand in the grass on the slope so everybody can see
the stage ok.

The guy gives his pitch about the bottles of medicine
first. How the ingredients come from Tibet and the
Amazon valley and how Dr. Dalton stumbled on the
formula while living with some headhunters near the
headwaters of the Amazon. The headhunters live to
be over 150 years old. He never explained how the
natives in the Amazon got the stuff from Tibet. Maybe
Dalton added that later. The bottles cost a dollar
apiece. We guys all chipped in and bought a bottle,

because we figured if they were putting on funny plays for free, we should pay our way too, or not watch. On the side of the bottle the label said:
Dr. W. Dalton's
LIVER MEDICINE
Guaranteed to Cure

Piles	Eruptions
Worms	Irisipilus
Scrofula	Scourges
Liver Complaint	Bilious Colic
Ague	Corrupt Humors
Dropsy	Flatulency
Dyspepsia	Gravel in the Urine
Scaly Skin	Painters Colic
Leprosy	Cholic Colon
Gout	The King's Evil in
Night Sweats	it's Worst Forms

The label scared the heck out of us so we each took a swallow. It tasted like Cascara. None of us had ever heard of the King's Evil. It must be something awful, but now we are all immune from it. I got to keep the bottle, cuz I put an extra 20 cents in the pot. I showed the bottle to dad when I got home. He said he had never heard of the King's Evil either and I'd better start realizing that just cuz a thing is printed on paper doesn't mean it's true. I said, "Does that mean that Tess of the Durbevilles might have been a liar and a cheat?" He looked at me sideways and said, "Come on."

May 8 Sunday

Had diarreah this morning and stayed home. Mom said I ought to be more careful about drinking patent medicines. I told her it tasted like Cascara and she said it was probably the most expensive laxitive I'd ever drink. Mom got out the family album for me to help while away the time between trips to the bathroom.

The high school's girl basketball team plays the preliminary games before the boy's games. Charlotte plays on the team, and several months ago the team griped about not having a fight song like the boys had. Their coach is John Strauss, who claims he is a direct descendant of Johann Sebastian Strauss. He said he would write one. He did. Here it is.

> Aren't they neat, ha, ha,
> sweet, ha, ha,
> winsome and fair.
> They're the Jim Dandies
> the boys all declare.
> They're all high rolling,
> rollicking swells.
> Here's to our girl's team,
> now don't they look well!

Charlotte said she thought it was the worst song ever penned by the hand of man. Well, the team thanked him and suggested the song be used for one year and then let someone else have the honor of writing one. That was pretty clever, huh?

May 13 Friday

After school today Fish and I were riding along State street when an airplane flew over. That was the first time we had ever seen an airplane. It was a biplane. It flew over Dr. Martin Luthern College and disappeared behind the trees on the other side of Summit avenue. We put on speed and finally came out on the meadow behind Herman's monument. There was the plane. We walked our bikes over some corn stubbles to the plane. The pilot was standing there looking around. We said Hi. He said Hi We said where did you come from? He said, Minneapolis. Took me about 45 minutes. Wow! It took us four hours in a car. We asked him what he was doing here and he said, "Well, I'm bringing in a Bat Man here for your 4th of July celebration. I take him up to 8000 feet. He bails out and glides around on a pair of canvas wings attached to his arms and legs until he gets down to about 2000 feet when he pulls the rip cord. He's supposed to land in front of the grandstand. I came down early to make sure I had a place to land and check out the the layout of the fairgrounds. "You kids want a ride? Cost you a buck apiece." We said we'd be right back. He said tell everybody that you see that I'm here giving rides, will you?" We said sure and off we tore.

We yelled at about 20 people on the way to get some money. They looked at us as if we were crazy. One guy yelled back, "What do you want me to do? Take him some gas?" People sure aren't interested in airplanes. Dad told me that when the Wright brothers were making flights of several minutes around Kitty Hawk, that people in the area weren't even interested enough to come out and watch. Once when a reporter from the New York Times came out the wind blew so hard they couldn't fly that day. So the brothers asked him to stay until the next day. The reporter said, "I've got to get back. I may come out next month." and then never came back, even though history was being made right at Kitty Hawk. People in general are not too smart.

We got our dollars and pumped up that blankety blank hill once more. There were several cars up there now and people were walking around the plane. The pilot was pouring gas into the plane from a five gallon tin. We peeked into the back cockpit. The instrument panel was a mess. Most of the instruments were smashed. There was an engine heat dial and a tacometer. Both the bank and turn indicator and the altimeter were busted. We gave him our two bucks and asked him how he could fly without instruments. He said,"Well, I can see how high I am. I can feel the turns and watch those little white rags tied on the wing struts so I don't get into a slide slip. The main thing is to watch the engine rev's so I don't get going too slow and stall. It's really easier than people think."

We helped him lift the tail and turn the plane around. He showed us where to step and we crawled up into the front cockpit. The plane was a Jenny with an Allison In-line engine. The pilot fiddled with his controls and then went out to the prop and gave it a few slow pumps. The he gave the prop a heck of a twist. The engine started right away, tac a tac a tac a tac a tac. He ran over to the cockpit, climbed in, revved up the engine a few times and off we trundled. Fish says, "Today is Friday the 13th."

We took off ok but I was surprised how bumpy the ride was. I always thought you'd glide along real smooth like, but not in this tub. He flew us in one big circle over Hauenstein's brewery, the Cottonwood dam, the Eagle Flour Mill and Herman's Monument. We could pick out our houses too. As we approached the cornfield to land the motor cut out. We both grabbed the edge of the cockpit. He yelled,"Don't panic. We glide in to land. Saves gas!" We flared out and then Bang, Bang we bounced in and rolled to a stop. We got out and Fish said, "Do you always drop a plane in like that?" He said,"I just bought it last month. This is only the 8th time I've landed it, but I'm getting better."

Ed Haugen asked Spot, Fish, Loyd and me if we'd like to drive out to Highmore, South Dakota, tomorrow. A friend of his had to drop out of college because his family had been pretty hard hit by the drought. Ed wanted to drive out and say hello to his friend Merril.

May 14 Saturday

We started out early. Went through Sleepy Eye, Tracy, Lake Benton and crossed the Minnesota border about 8 am. Ed had a second- hand green Auburn with yellow wooden spoke wheels. We did pretty well until we got about 50 miles beyond Brookings when we had a flat. The wheels had detachable metal rims, so we loosened 4 lug nuts, slipped off the rim and tire and put the spare on in about 5 minutes. We had one more spare.

Minnesota had been green, wet and lush with white picket fences and trees and crops just starting out of the ground everywhere. But as soon as we hit South Dakota it wasn't 20 miles before the green had change to gray sand. The sand was everywhere. In dunes, blowing across the road and even in the air like a low lying fog about two feet above the ground. We passed dried carcasses of cows and dead trees without a leaf on them. The dust bowl was everywhere. Merril lived in Highmore in the middle of South Dakota. We pulled into town about 1 pm. The temperature was about 100 degrees. Most of the houses had boards over the windows. There wasn't a car moving anywhere. We found Merril's house and knocked. Merril invited us in. It was dark inside. Three of Merril's friends were sitting around a table stripped to the waist. A pitcher of ice water was sitting on the table. They'd been playing bridge.

We stayed for only about an hour. Merril said his dad was making $14 a week working at a garage, but people could hardly afford gasoline, so there wasn't much business. His mom was volunteering at the Food Center. The federal government was trucking in food like milk, eggs, butter and flour. The wells had dried up so water was brought in by tank trucks. People went to the trucks each morning to fill up their containers. We could hardly believe such a difference existed between our town and his within a distance of 300 miles.

Merril said it was just as bad the farther west or south you went, and was caused by several things. Farmers had not rotated crops over a long period of time and the nitrogen in the soil finally gave out. Also counties had drained swamps that usually stored water, to make more farm land. Dams were built for irrigation but silted up. When the drought started the rivers began drying up and BANG you've got a desert. He said there was one advantage, there were no flies. Eh,eh. But then there were no birds either.

We said goodbye. I can still see the four guys standing in the road in the hot sun smiling and yelling goodbye with the sand blowing across their shoe tops. Nobody said much on the way home. We hit the green Minnesota border about sundown. Ed said, "You know, the planet can sure go to hell in a hand basket if you don't take care of it."

May 15 Sunday

Got to Sunday school and guess what? That's right. Another new teacher, Mrs. Stone. We said, "Where's Jim?" She said, "He won't be teaching this class anymore." We all said, "Why not?" And she says,"Well, we understand he's been telling you boys that all religions are the same. He's obviously not a true Christian." I said, "Who's we?" and she said, "The Women's Auxilliary." Fish said, "Well, I think the Women's Auxilliary is stupid!" and got up and walked out. I was half way out of my chair to follow him when I figured I'd better stay so I could tell dad all the details. Ifigured this was something we needed adult help on.

We got her to explain more what she meant. Then we told her what Jim had really told us. We gave her some of the examples Jim had told us about. Then we argued that just because Jim had given us something interesting to think about, he wasn't qualified to teach us.? She wasn't too sure of why they had fired Jim, and I don't think she knew much about religious history either. Gee, Jim had been all over the world and had a masters in Humanities or something. We asked her if she could name any of the other Sunday school teachers who had dragged a tree off Henrietta's roof or done any other act of kindness with the class. We had her stumped there. By the time class was over I think we had won.

When we got outside we all agreed to tell our folks that something had to be done to get Jim back or by God with a capital G we were not going back to Sunday school, period. It was the first time we were all mad at the same time. JR said he didn't think Mrs. Stone had ever been farther away from town than Hanska... well, maybe Mankato, he would allow. That wasn't too funny, but that"s JR.

Hal Soukup was giving us some more coaching this afternoon and said that this summer he'd like to get together a tennis team and play different towns around southern Minnesota. Boy, we thought that would be great. Our folks have come through with some better rackets. I got a Top-Flite. It is the first one we've seen that has an open throat. Looks real sharp. Hal was helping us on the serve and suddenly went into one of his comedy routines.

"Bring the racket over the right shoulder with the elbow cocked. Keeping one eye on the ball, the other on the opponent, make certain the upper arm between the shoulder and the elbow is pointed at the North Star. This is true only in the northern hemisphere. Now throw the head of the racket at the ball remembering to squeeze the handle with your right hand while removing your fingers from the ball in your left hand to avoid abrasions. Keeping your weight off your feet, run rapidly toward the net with toes pointed at the right sideline, always remembering to keep the racket clear of the ground.

We all about died laughing.

Then he said,"Gather around fellows, I want to pass on to you some tactics I've learned over the years. If a real rich family invites you to play on their private court, and you want to play there again, here are a few tips:

1. Serve short to their forehand.
2. Serve one double fault each game.
3. Use low short lobs.
4. When receiving keep your feet together with your weight on your heels.
5. Stand close to the service line when receiving.
6. Practice your high top-spin drop shots.

They were funny. But they also made us think about feet apart, weight forward,etc. He's pretty foxy.

During supper I told mom and dad about Jim. I was getting pretty hot under the collar the more I talked. At the end dad said,"Well, I'm pretty certain we'll get Jim back. Take it easy for a few days and let me see what I can do by talking with a few of the church elders. It was foolish to replace him without hearing his side for one thing. And besides he is one hell of a nice guy. Between you and me I'd much rather have Jim teaching you kids than anyone I know in the whole town, believe me."

I felt a lot better just hearing dad say that. But things can sure happen quick. I hope there's a silver lining to this one.

May 20 Friday

We all went to the movie tonight. It was about a racehorse, Broadway Bill. These two young people had raised him from a colt and raced him at county fairs for fun. But one morning when they were giving him a workout he ran the mile and a quarter in two minutes and 2 seconds, or something like that, which, I guess, is pretty good time, because the girl and boy did a lot of jumping up and down. Now, of course, they had to get him in a big purse race. So the rest of the picture was them towing Bill around in a rickety trailer with an old truck, keeping him warm with their own blankets when rain leaked into his rotting stall and buying him oats and hay while they went without supper. All they needed to make it a real tear jerker was a blind old man, a crippled kid on a crutch and a dog with only three legs. However, they finally get the money together for the entry fee into the big race and a jockey. But crooked gamblers bribe the jockey at the last minute into throwing the race because the gamblers know that Broadway Bill will beat the fetlocks off the horse they bet on.

They come out of the gate, and slowly but surely Bill starts moving up in the pack. The crooked jockey lets him get up near the front and then starts pulling in on the reins. But Broadway Bill manages to get the bit in his teeth as they come around the clubhouse turn into the home stretch and keeps right on gaining on the leader. Now the jockey really starts hauling back on the reins. But now the theater audience starts getting into the act. They start booing and yelling, "Come on, Baby!" right out loud in the theater. One lady down in front jumps to her feet. The guy behind her jumps up too. Then the guy behind him climbs up on his seat. Then everybody jumps up and starts yelling at the top of their lungs. "Come on, Billy Boy! Come on, Baby!" We kids couldn't see, so we piled out in the aisle and stood there. Well, the horses come pounding down the stretch with the jockey yanking on the reins and Broadway Bill shaking his head and running like mad. He isn't going to let these kids down. (The kids are married now.) With a super effort he manages a last burst of speed, noses out the leader at the wire and collapses in the dirt, throwing the mean jockey over his head.

Myrna Loy runs across the track and holds the horses head in her arms. Everybody in the theater stumbles back to their seats sort of sheepish like. The women get out their handkerchiefs and have a good cry, while the men pretend to clean their glasses or blow their nose. What a finish! I never liked Mickey Rooney after that. He was the crooked jockey. They had to shoot Broadway Bill. They should have shot Mickey Rooney.

May 21 Saturday

Tom had ordered our troop some lemonwood staves to make bows. They came yesterday and today we started shaving them down with spokeshaves. We used a storage room off the gym at Turner Hall and by noon we were a foot deep in shavings, but we had some pretty good looking bows about 5 to 6 feet long with maybe 25 to 40 pound pulls. Then we used pieces of broken beer bottle glass to scrape down the bumps plus fine sandpaper until the surface was like glass.

NOCKS FOR
BOWSTRING

You leave the handle (the thick part) below the center of the bow, so when the arrow slides over the top of your fist it is in the center of the bow.

Tom had shown us how to beeswax a skein of fine linen threads together. You take 3 of these skeins and lay them clockwise over each other while you twist each skein counterclockwise until you have a six foot long bowstring.

Goose brought some turkey feathers, which we stripped off the quill, cut them to feather shapes,

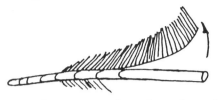

and glued them down on the dowel ends with fletching glue and pins. The dowels are 30 inches long.

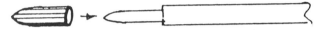

Then we fitted the metal points on.

Cut the nock at 90 degrees to the cock feather, and we had an arrow. We made six each.

The reason you make the nock at 90 degrees to the cock feather is so that when the arrow is released the other two feathers slide over the bow handle without knocking the arrow out of line.

It took several days to varnish the bow and arrows and paint our trade marks on each arrow, etc. We already had cuff guards, because we had archery at school, but we had never made all the gunsa-ga-schmeer ourselves.

May 22 Sunday

Our Sunday scool class didn't meet today. We were sent to another class. Dad said that there is quite a flap going on between the Women's Auxilliary, the Board of Elders, the reverend Younger and whoever wants to get in on the argument, he gathers. There is a meeting at the church tonight, and Jim has been asked to come. I sure hope he goes and just doesn't think to heck with it. That would be awful. Dad isn't home yet from the meeting, so I'll have to wait until tomorrow to find out what happened.

This afternoon we all helped Tom get ready for the Memorial Day program at the fairgrounds next Sunday. Toots Thompson, the elecrician, took some of us to the armory where we picked up 3 army tents and lugged them on to the truck. At Turner Hall we stacked some flats together from the stage and folded up a few of the platform risers they use for the choir and got them on the truck. Then we all wrestled the piano from the gym up the stairs, out through the card room to the truck and got it roped down. I played "The Twelfth Street Rag" for the guys and I wasn't too bad. I kept forgetting the ending and had to start over again until they made me quit. Miss Christenson says I'll probably polish it up by the end of the school year, and then I'll be free of "The Little Elfin's March" forever. She's pretty neat.

May 25th Wednesday

Jim will be back, dad told me last night. Hooray! What a silver lining that is!

The Chamber of Commerce put on a dinner and program in the Turner Hall theater and stage this evening. They push the seats back under the dress circle and put tables around a little dance floor in front of the stage. Half the town turns out to see the skits and hear the Barber Shop Singers.

They had a gag they wanted pulled off and they needed two guys who could hang from the balcony railing without falling off. The Chamber guys are mostly business men who are overweight and don't spend much time doing chin ups or giant swings in their office. Tom suggested Loyd and me. Ernie Herrigan told us how the gag would work.

Loyd would be dressed up as a girl at a table near the door. We dressed a dummy in his exact same clothes and laid it down in the front row of the balcony so nobody could see it. The balcony is empty. They don't use it for eating. They got me dressed up with a mustache and a black wig like a gigilo. In the middle of dinner, I walk up to Miss Loyd and start to annoy her. She tells me to go away in a falsetto voice getting louder and louder, until finally she hits me over the head with her purse. I grab the purse and run through the tables with Miss Loyd in hot pursuit. At the top of the stairway to the balcony we've put two metal garbage cans. As we run up the stairs we knock these over. They make a heck of a noise so everybody looks up at the balcony.

I run down to the front row in the balcony by the rail, where Loyd catches up to me and we pretend to wrestle. First I push Loyd over the rail and he hangs on the railing with one hand, but manages to climb back up and then forces me backward until I'm hanging by my knees while Loyd holds my feet with his knees. By this time the diners are all looking up and wondering whether it's a gag or not. Now I give Loyd a push and he falls down out of sight alongside the dummy and out of sight of the audience. I reach down, pick up the dummy, hold it over my head for effect, and then toss it over the rail where it plummets down through the crepe paper streamers and lands in the center of the dance floor, SQUASH! A siren sounds off stage. Women scream...They really didn't expect the dummy. Two men in white coats rush in with a stretcher, toss the dummy on it, and rush off, while the siren fades into the distance.

That gag sets the stage for the rest of the evening.

May 29 Sunday

Still no Jim, but dad says don't worry, Jim will
definitely be back, but they have to take a little time
to let some people apologize or save face, whatever
that means. Being grown up must be awful
complicated.

May 30th, Monday, is Memorial Day, but the pageant
is put on tonight so people can get drunk and not
have to go to work the next morning. We worked all
day. We put up the army tents, covered two corn
husking wagons with lath and canvas so they looked
like Canastoga Wagons. Made a Confederate flag and a
pile of fake cannon balls to put beside the French 75
cannon the Veterans of Foreign Wars hauled down.

The pageant lasts for two hours, from 8 to 10. It
showed parts of all the wars. There are scads of old
mouldy uniforms and costumes in the Turner Hall
dressing rooms, so everybody gets decked out. Even
if the sleeves are half way up the arm and the coats
don't button, nobody can see this from the
grandstand. Besides the horses galloping across the
baseball diamond raise so much dust, nobody can see
anything anyhow.

It starts with the Indians fighting the settlers and
the government troops. The Indians and Cavalry
gallop across from left to right. Then the
revolutionary war part comes with English soldiers
falling right and left while Yorktown, carboard
silhouettes, gets blasted with fireworks left over
from last year's Fourth of July. Yorktown is burned to
the ground, but the wind is toward the grandstand
and the smoke rolls over the audience for about ten
minutes before they get Yorktown put out.

Some of the town toughs were a little soused and
yelled, "To hell with freedom. Put that blankety

blank fire out!" This made some sober guys mad, and they started a free for all right on the edge of section G. But Herb Hackbart and Sherlock Holm, the two town policemen, were up there in a minute and threw two or three of the drunks down a couple of empty rows. Then everybody sat and watched the pageant again.

The Civil War was next. It was the Battle of Gettysberg. The confederate cavalry galloped across from right to left and met the Union Army at third base. There was a lot of horses rearing, guys pretending to club each other and saber waving. Then the Confederates turned and galloped back from left to right into the dark. The high school football coach led the Confederate Cavalry. He got two front teeth knocked out.

The World War was next. This time there was just the American flag up on the flagpole with a spotlight on it and a platoon of Veterans of Foreign Wars and American Legion guys in their real uniforms doing some close order drills. Then Mrs. O'Malley stood by the piano and sang The Star Spangled Banner through a megaphone.

It was close to midnight by the time we got everything picked up. We hoisted the piano on the bed of a stake truck. Spot had his license, so they told him to drive the truck up to his uncle's garage and leave it there until morning when somebody would come get it. Loyd, Fish and I went along.

As soon as we got away from the fair grounds I started to play "The Twelfth Street Rag" and we decided to drive back and forth down all the streets to give the town a seranade. We drove down Washington street to the south side park and back on State to 5th north, down to Broadway south to the Union Hospital and then down to Minnesota street and along the main drag. As we went along the lights in all the houses would come on as people wondered where the music was coming from. Fish kept track. I played it 22 times. We got about halfway along the main drag when Herb Hackbart came alongside on his 4 cylinder Henderson and motioned Spot over to the curb. He said, "All right, you funny fellows. You've wakened the entire town. Now chill it and go home or I'll tell your dads and you'll be quarantined for a month. And Billy, for God's sake, tell Miss Christenson I'll pay her anything to teach you another piece!" Herb is scoutmaster of the other troop in town. He is funny. But we did what he told us.

June 3 Friday

Jerry came home from the U this weekend. In the last few months he's been getting a jazz orchestra together, so they can play at dance halls around southern Minnesota this summer and make some extra money. They call it the Orient Dance Band.

They practiced tonight for the first time in our living room. Jerry is on the piano, plus drums, trumpet, trombone, two clarinets, a sax and a bass horn. Jerry can also play the steel guitar, piano accordian, banjo and oboe. We kids sat outside on the porch steps and listened to Dardenella, The Maple Leaf Rag, Japanese Sandman, Just a Cottage Small, Kitten on the Keys, etc. Pretty soon half the neighborhood was sitting on our front lawn. When had a rest, mom and dad brought out pitchers of lemonade and cookies for everybody. The cookies were vanilla wafers with marshmallow cream inside a chocolate covering. Dad always brings a whole case home, because he says those are his favorite fruit.

They stopped playing at 9:30. Mom said, "I can't understand what you see in that stuff. If there is a melody you keep breaking it up. Then you mangle and shred it. It's only a bunch of noise to me." She plays records like Peer Gynt Suite and Hungarian Rhapsody Number 2 on the victrola.

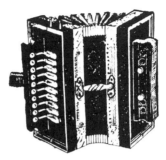

June 4 Saturday

It has turned real warm the last few days. We've been playing a lot of tennis after school and then biking out to the Cottonwood Dam to go swimming in the evenings. The dam is half concrete and half wood that is rotting away. The old mill wheel is still there in the concrete flume on the side , but most of the river pours over the wood part and scours out a pool about 40 feet in diameter just below the dam.

We do most of our swimming and diving in the pool, because up stream the river winds through pasture lands. The cows stand in the water to cool and the cow pies come floating down the river. So if you swim above the dam you have to use the breast stroke to keep from getting hit in the face. But when the cow pies go over the dam they get pulverized, so you don't notice them.

You can dive off the flume which is about 15 feet high or off the wooden part which is lower. The pool is shallower by the flume. You have to hit the water at a 45 degree angle so you don't hit the bottom and break your neck. One other thing is annoying. There are planks sticking out from the wooden part we dive off of. But to the left are several posts or piles that stick up out of the water in summer but are submerged during the spring floods. You don't want to dive to the left.

After tennis this afternoon we were starting to bike out Broadway to the dam when Herb tore by on his Henderson, and a few minutes later Doc Reinecke's Air-Flow Chrysler came past doing 65 at least. Doc is the county coroner, so we put on some speed and got out to the dam about ten minutes later.

Herb was standing over a body, in a black swim suit, lying on the sand bar about 100 feet below the dam. Three other boys that we didn't know were standing there also. Doc was on his knees beside the body. We went up. It was the first time any of us had seen a dead body. The boy's skull had an inch wide crack completely across the head and part of the brain was hanging out. Herb looked up and shooed us away.

We asked the boys what happened. They said they had come from some farms south of town to go

swimming but hadn't taken time to check out the pool before they dived in. Their friend had dived to the left and hit a pile six inches under water head on.

Then the ambulance got there, and they put the body in. It was a grayish blue.

All of a sudden I got cold all over and this picture flashed into my mind. The arc light going out in a big flash and the guys running away in the dark laughing.

June 5 Sunday

One more week of school. Hot dog. Graduation Thursday night. There's a new haircut we guys are getting. It's called a crew cut. Instead of side burns and hair parted on the side, the barber cuts the top flat about an inch long and runs the clipper straight up the sides. It's sure a relief not to have hair hanging in your eyes when you do a handstand. When we were in the bathroom this morning dad tapped me on the shoulder with his comb and said, "Billy, why don't you let your hair grow like regular men?" I told him all the kids were wearing crew cuts. He sort of sighed and said, "Well, I suppose the cycle will come around again in about thirty years." I said, "What cycle?" And he said, "The hirsute cycle." Whatever that meant.

Sunday school. And Jim was back like dad said. We all stood up and cheered when he came in. Jim said,"I want to thank you guys. You really are something. Amazing!"

We got talking about heroes today. Jim asked us what heroes we had, if any. We mainly had movie characters like Tony Moreno in "Mare Nostrum" who sank the German sub just before he went under. Jim said those people do symbolize our ideals, but did it ever occur to us that those characters were only pretending to be heroes? I guess we hadn't thought about it that much. Jim asked us to name a few people we thought were real heroes. We named George Washington, Abraham Lincoln and a few

116

others and then we were able to cough up Betsy Ross, Florence Nightingale and Joan of Arc and that was about it. Then he said, "Do any of you have any heroes that you know personally?" We all thought a while. All of a sudden Fish said," Yeah. You." I think that kind of surprised Jim because he said,"Well..thanks Fish..really."

We gabbed some more about how people get all excited about movie stars, mob them for autographs and scream when they go by. When you think about it lot of idiots go ga-ga over celluloid images who are only acting. Jim asked us if we knew the names of any movie writers. Nobody did. How come nobody jumps up and down and asks writers and directors for their autographs? They are really the brains. Without writers the actors wouldn't exist. Wierd, huh?

We ended up with another assignment that was interesting instead of a stupid chore like memorizing the capitols of all the states. Jim suggested we talk to our folks or older people around town and ask them who they thought were outstanding citizens or heroes in this area. Also try to get any information or anecdotes they could recall about these persons. We told him again how great it was to have him back, and off we went into the cruel, cruel world, girding up our loins, manning the battlements and holding our banners on high.

When I told dad about our assignment I asked him why Jim's assignments always seemed fun to do, while most of the assignments in school were so dumb. Dad said that Jim gave us problems to solve that were interesting to our ages, and then tried to get us to come up with a principle. You know, it's almost as important to know what to forget as it is to remember what's important. And along that line, Jim tries to get you guys to think and formulate your own principles. Heck, anybody can look up facts, why memorize 'em?

That's why we all got Jim back. He's a modern day Socrates. Even better. Because first he finds out what you kids are interested in. Once he found that out he started asking you questions that he knew would interest you. He's also fun and enthusiastic. Actually, Bill, the real definition of education is to become enthusiastic and curious. Training merely means you memorize what other people have learned. And I feel there are too many teachers out there that train kids; stuff them full of facts; and never let them realize that they have brains that can solve, as well as memorize."

Dad paused then, and said,"Well, that was some lecture, but you asked the question and I presume you got the answer." "I sure did, dad," I said, "It means I don't have to memorize the multiplication tables any more." He gives me that sideways look, grabs my neck and pretends to choke me to death.

June 9 Thursday

Went right home after school cuz I had to cut the front yard. None of the gang was around, so when I put the lawnmower in the garage, I started poking around the shelves for something to do. I found an old tin machine gun that used to be Jerry's and a clip of wooden bullets. It had a tripod too. I wiped the dust off, oiled the crank and shoved the clip into the receiver top. I put the gun in the garage door , so I wouldn't hit anything in the garage and gave the crank about five fast cranks and shot five holes in our sunroom window. Holy Moses, I didn't think they'd go that far...Just then Fish came around the house. He lives behind us across the alley and sometimes takes a short cut through our yard. He said, "How

come you weren't at graduation rehearsal?" I said,
"Oh my God. That's where everybody was. Did they
take role?" "Nope", said Fish, "But they did count
heads for some reason."

I showed Fish the machine gun. Then I showed him
the sunroom window. He said,"You know, you and I
could rob the Citizen's State Bank with this heater."
We both laughed.

I had to put on a necktie for graduation. It was on
the stage at Turner Hall, because the High School
Graduation was being held at the high school
auditorium.

This evening we were all back stage and seated
alphabetically from the A's in front to Wayne Walstrub
in the last row on the end. No Bockus was called so I
hung around Wayne. I figured out now they counted
heads so Hank Crane, the janitor, would set up the
right number of chairs. Everybody sat. So I bent my
knees and squatted beside Wayne. Just about the
time my legs started to quiver under the strain,
Hank saw from the wings that I didn't have a chair.
So he went Ps-s-st, and motioned to me that he
would push a folding chair to me under the back
drop. Cuz he didn't want to walk out on the stage.
Okay, he pushed the chair under the back drop, but
he forgot the rose trellis was leaning against the
drop. When I crawled on my belly back to get the
chair, the trellis fell over, crash right on me and
knocked Wayne over too. Well, Harry Daggart came
running over. There I was looking up at him from
the floor all covered with paper roses. His lips
started to quiver. Then he said, "God!" and walked
back to the podium. Hank got us squared away in a
jiffy and everybody got their diploma. I was the last
one to be called and when I started across the apron
I noticed JR sitting in the front row. Now JR is the
wierd one in our gang. Once he sucked up and drank

a whole mud puddle on a dare for forty cents. I knew he hadn't forgotten that BB shot in his leg and he'd probably try to trip me. Sure enough, I saw his eyes look down toward my feet. He tried to kick my heel over my other ankle, but I jumped up in the air, turned, and stamped on his toe. He didn't yell, but I know he felt it good. It got a good laugh out of the audience. Harry was smiling too as he handed me my diploma. His face looked like Lon Chaney when Cristine tore off his phantom mask by the pipe organ. He said, "You'll never know how happy I am to see you graduate."

Then a gray-haired man gave a long speech. The guys in front had to sit still, but Wayne and I played rock, scissors, paper. Wayne won 64 to 58. The man's final words were,"He seen his duty and he done it noble. Angels could have did no more." Harry thanked him and said he would carry those words to the grave with him. Then everybody clapped and came up on the stage where they shook the boys hands and kissed the girls.

June 10 Friday

Something wierd happened last night after graduation. About midnight I awoke and heard a noise out by the garage. My bedroom is at the back of the house over the sunroom and has a door leading out to a small balcony. The door was open cuz it was warm. I looked out and there was a man trying to get into the garage door. I got my bow, strung it, nocked an arrow, and took a bead on the garage door about 6 feet from the guy's head. Just as I released I thought, my God, I forgot the wind. There was a only a light breeze, but it was enuf to put the arrow in the door about two feet from his head. THUNK! He took one look at the arrow and took off. But I was more scared than he was. I sat on the edge of my bed and thought, what if I had killed him? Boy, that's the last time I'm going to do anything like that in a hurry. It took me five minutes before I stopped shaking. That was another dumb one. That's three strikes today. Bullets, roses and near death. Harry was right. I'm cersed.

June 11 Saturday

This morning I was watching dad go thru his mail. About every other one he would toss in the wastebasket without opening it. I said, "How do you know which one's to throw away?" Dad said, "I'm psychic. Try me." So I opened one in the wastebasket and told him the return address. He said, "The insurance company wants me to take out more life insurance, and the first three months are free if I do it before June 31." I said, "It's 4 months free." He said, "Irrelevant. Next." I said Ford Motor Company." He said,"They're advertising their new Model A with automatic starter." I said, "With automatic spark advance." He said, "Obvious necessity. Next." I said, "Kraft Cheese Company." He said,"They are packing four different cheeses in 1/4, 1/2 and pound packages plus a five pound carton with a promotion discount of 20 percent the first purchase." I said, "Perfect. How did you know?" He said, "That's my business. Remember?" "Here's a tough one" I said,"The state Republican party." He said, "they want me to phone 5 people on voting day this November. They want a $25 donation. They want me to vote for Hoover for president." Wow, he sure is psychic. Those guys in the medicine show that held envelopes up to their foreheads and tell the sudience what's in them have nothing on dad. He doesn't even have to hold them up to his forehead.

Fish and I went over to Judge Gislason's home this evening to play chess. Al Fredricks was there and Shorty, the editor of the Brown County Journal. Three other men were there too. The judge was on a kick of playing knight to Queen two instead of to

Bishop three, which is standard play. He claimed it made for a tighter defense and confused the opponent by not always playing the standard opening. We played about two games apiece from 7 to 10. Then the judge and Al decided to play one more quickie at five seconds per move. Each guy would move and then count slowly to 5 and the other guy had to make his move before the other guy said five. The game went like this:

Fredricks	Gislason
White	Black

1. P-K4	P-QB3
2. P-Q4	P-Q4
3. Kt-QB3	PxKP
4. KtxP	Kt-Q2
5. Q-K2	KKt-B3
6. Kt-Q6 Mate	

The judge didn't check on Als5th move. It looked meaningless, but Al never makes meaningless moves.

That didn't set too well with the judge, so they played one more quickie.

Gislason	Fredricks
White	Black

1. P-Q4	Kt-KB3
2. Kt-Q2	P-K4
3. PxP	Kt-Kt5
4. P-KR3	Kt-K6 Judge resigned or:
5. PxKt	Q-R5 Check
6. P-Kt2	QxP Mate

The judge stopped playing Kt-Q2 from then on. But I learned something from him. He is much older than the other guys and I can see how he gets tired playing the same old openings. After that I started trying different ways of bringing out my pieces and had a lot more fun, because unless a player was much stronger than I, it would confuse the heck out of him. I learned to play better by attacking outrageously, even though I lost in 14 or 15 moves. You stop worrying so much about winning and see how fast you can get the other guy. So you lose in 3 minutes. You start another game, and each time you learn about chess instead of memorizing fifty variation moves on a single opening that every grandmaster has to memorize and play or he gets his butt beat. For us ordinary kids, that's boring.

June 12, Sunday

Well, we brought in quite a few heroes. Names of local people who had done remarkable things. One guy had won a bronze star. One gal saved Vic Schroeder's life when he fell through the ice in the Minnesota River years ago. I guess he was destined to fall off or into things. One older man had paid the way thru college of 4 boys and 2 girls anonymously and he's still anonymous. Paul Scheffer of all people had been on a government team that helped reactivate Interpol police organization in 1923. One old lady in her 80's had stumped the town to raise money for the foundation of the Union Hospital way back when. A bachelor farmer with no kin had willed his farm to the town with the stipulation that it be made into a golf course. That's where our golf course came from. I brought in the one about Doc Howard and the little girl out at the poor house. We had a total of 32 people who certainly deserved the title of hero with a lot more reason than movie stars. We talked about it and wondered why these people had almost gone unnoticed. We finally came to the conclusion that real heroes didn't do things to be noticed; they did what they did, because they wanted to and that was that.

We agreed the real heroes weren't known because they were almost everywhere and never would be well known. Jim certainly changed our idea of what a hero is. Check out your friends, your town or even your mom and dad before you go screaming after Hoot Gibson or Constance Talmadge.

Then Jim says, "Do people have to do exceptional, remarkable things to be heroes?" Ye Gods, we just think we've got something settled when he starts us thinking again.

This afternoon we played our first town tennis match with Granite Falls. We played at the Southside Park courts. By 3 in the afternoon it was 102 degrees and humid. The match was tied and I had to win my match against a man in his fifties. He beat me the first set 6-1, and had me 4-2 in the second, when he turned pale, staggered up to the net and said he would have to default and fell over. Gosh, we carried him over to the shade and called the hospital. They were there in a minute and the ambulance driver said he was probably suffering from heat exhaustion cuz his face was pale. If it was sunstroke his face would have been red as a beet.

It wasn't much satisfaction winning the match that way. So we all trooped over to the hospital and talked with the Granite Falls team until the guy felt better. They all left then but we will play them at Granite Falls next summer.

June 15 Wednesday

Loyd, Spot, Fish and I and Jimmy, a kid who lives near Spot, were standing with our bikes in front of Al Fredricks bar this morning when a Model T Ford came around the corner and ran, bang, into the side of a big Stork Co. egg truck parked by the curb. The Model T tipped over and the driver slid out across the street. He didn't seem mad. He walked over to where we were standing and said,"I've had that wreck for 15 years. The front wheels keep jacknifing on me. One of these days it's going to get me. I'll sell it, as is, for a dollar. Any takers?" We all yelled,"We'll take it!" and started to pool our change, when Vic Leash said,"Boys, you're going to need another ten bucks for the registration fee." Vic has a little office a block away where he handles property deeds, car registrations, Power of Attorney papers, and notarizes stuff.

We all tore home, got our $2.20 and came back. Then Vic, the farmer and we five went down to Vic's office. Spot was the only one with a driver's license so he signed for it. We gave the farmer his dollar, and we had a car lying on its side in the middle of the street that wouldn't run. Wow!

The guys in the bar helped us tip it back up. We pushed it south on Broadway and then up second street to Jimmy's garage in the alley. The windshield was smashed so we unbolted it. We found an old four by four, laid it across the rafters above the engine and rigged up a block and tackles sort of to lift the engine out if we had to. We fooled around all afternoon polishing it up. We tried to start it by cranking it but it wouldn't turn over. We finally all went home for supper.

June 16,17, 17 Thu.,Fri.,Sat.

Played tennis in the morning. Worked on car in afternoon.

June 19 Sunday

Finally got it running. Cuggy Nieman, a mechanic at Martinka's garage had been one of the guys that helped us tip the T upright. He dropped by Thursday after work to see if he could help us out. He figured out that everything seemed to be working but not enough spark to keep it going. So he had us take the magneto apart. Sure enough, some of the contacts were jimmied out of place. He went back to his garage and brought back the parts and helped us get them in place. He said we could put it back together and if we needed more help holler. However, he said not to ask him to risk his neck test driving it. Eh,eh,eh.

We got the magneto plate just about bolted in place when Jimmy dropped one of the nuts down in the magneto. So we had to take it all apart and start over again. Guess what? Yeah. He dropped the nut in the second time. How butterfingers can you get? Anyhow we got him out of there and finally got it back together. Jimmy's uncle gave us a Chevy windshield, so we forgave Jimmy and let him touch the car again. It was about six inches too wide. so we bent the side bars inward and bolted it on anyway. We took the cushion out of the back seat and sat on the boards. Otherwise we would sit up too high. The tires were shot. Again Jimmy's uncle came thru with four old Chevy tires. They were too large to fit the T so we squeezed them on over the T's tires, bored holes in the sidewalls and laced rope back and forth across the wheels to keep them from slipping around when we drove. It was pretty hard riding, but we didn't have to worry about flats.

We got all the used oil we wanted from the gas stations and kept a five gallon tin of it on the floor boards in the back seat. We use a quart about every 35 miles but it means we can spend our money on gas at 15 cents a gallon instead. There's no top so we keep two umbrellas. They work ok if you don't go over 10 miles an hour.

We drove to Lake Crystal today on our first trip. It's 25 miles away, but there's a fair beach and they have a diving board up on a tower about seven feet high. We practiced one and a half gainers all day. The board didn't have much snap to it, so you had to take a high hurdle and then wait it out until it threw you up. We'd taken along sweatshirts, because when you go from a full gainer to a one and a half you come around too late once in a while and land on your back. Oo-o-o does that smack and sting. We got so most of us could get our hands in before we blew it and then we started getting tired, so we quit, bought Eskimo Pies and went home. We decided to put the cushion back in the back seat after bouncing around on the wooden seat all day, looks or no looks.

June 20 Monday

Our whole family took off for Green Lake for a two week stay. Dad bought a cottage on Crescent Beach near Spicer. We've gone there the last several summers. I hated to leave the Model T and the gang but that's life. When I got there I looked up Jimmy Nichols who lived down the beach a ways. His dad and my dad are old friends from when they were in the lumbering business in Northern Minnesota years ago.

June 21 Tuesday

Dad had been trying to get a well digger named Harry from Spicer to come out all summer and dig us a new well near the kitchen door so we wouldn't have to walk so far to the old pump. This morning this older man shows up with a forked stick which he holds in his fists, fingers upward and starts witching for water. Pretty soon all the kids on the beach are standing around watching. Kids love magic. As we watched, I started to point out to Harry that the water level in front of the cottage was even with the water in the ditch at the back of our property, so why was he....why was he....Dad took my arm and walked me slowly into the kitchen and said, "Look, Willy, I've been trying to get a well dug since last fall. You know and I know and everybody on this lake knows, with the possible exception of those under four and the insane, that water exists about 15 or 20 feet down anywhere in northern Minnesota. But if this guy wants to play with his willow wand, let him. In fact, a few Oh's and Ah's from you wouldn't hurt any."

So I went back out, kept my mouth shut and watched the old guy pussy foot around until, lo and behold, the handle of the forked stick bent downward and pointed at the ground exactly where dad wanted the well put. It's amazing how many of the old fashioned techniques put modern technology to shame.
One thing puzzled me though. When the wand pointed at the ground, Harry turned, looked at me over his glasses and winked.

June 24 Friday

Jimmy had been building a diving helmet out of the top of an old water heater. A welder in Spicer had cut out shoulder holes and a square for the face plate. I helped Jimmy edge the shoulders with pieces of bicycle tires and put the glass face plate in with putty and bolts. Then we attached a long piece of garden hose to one of the pipe openings at the top and sealed off the other opening. We hooked the hose into a tire pump, so when we pumped, the air would bubble out the bottom.

We took it out on the Nichols raft in about eight feet of water. Jimmy put it on and lowered himself over the edge while I pumped. It worked ok but the water level in the helmet almost covered your mouth, so you had to tilt your head back to breathe. When you walked, your feet felt like they were going to float up in front of you, so we learned to lean forward and sort of push the heavy helmet ahead of us. All the kids on the beach wanted to try it, so Jimmey and I spent all afternoon on the raft pumping. Boy, were my shoulders red when we quit. Mom put some Unguentine on them.

June 26 Sunday

Not too much to write about. There is a pet crow that hangs around our cottage. He stores nuts, pieces of silver paper, gum wrappers and anything that is shiny under the edges of the shingles on our roof. When you look at the roof it looks like a flat Christmas tree. When the winds blows hard from across the lake he flies up to a small maple tree by the beach and hangs on to the top of it with one claw and lets himself blow around in the wind. The tree is bent way over with this dumb crow fluttering around like a bunch of black ribbons. Dad says that's probably the way they get rid of lice, but I think he does it just for fun. He'll come up and take food right out of your hand.

June 28 Tuesday

Dad asked me if I'd like to go horseback riding today. I said, "Not particularly." He said,"Aw, come on. Nobody else wants to go either." So I said ok and we drove over to Indian Point. On the way it started to rain. I thought, good, that'll kill the horsebacking. But, oh no. When dad sets out to do something, it's done. Indian Point is sort of a resort with a small roller coaster, a beach, cafe and horses. The man saddled two horses and helped me up. I felt as if I was sitting on a big barrel. The cowboys in the movies always look as if their legs go straight down on each side of the horse. Maybe they stand up all the time.

Anyhow we had a half hour ride in the rain yet. I had to keep kicking my mare to keep her going. She kept trying to turn around and go back. She had more sense than dad did. Then it started coming down in buckets, so dad turned around. When I turned her around she took off like a scared rabbit and galloped full speed back to the barn. Instead of going into the barn, she galloped right out into the barnyard and stood in the middle of a big mud puddle.

I tried jerking the reins, kicking her sides, patting her neck, slapping her butt, nothing worked. She just stood there grinning. I could hardly see the barn for the rain. What fun! Finally I saw the guy coming out of the surf, He was sliding along on two barrel staves. He put me over his shoulder and we squished back to the barn. I said to him,"Does she always do this?" And he said, "Always. Why do you think I invented these mud skiis?" "To ski down Mount Everest on a clear day with Sir Hillary over your shoulder?" I answered. He laughed and set me down in the barn.

We sloshed out to the car and squashed into the front seat. It was pouring rain and when we drove past the driveway to our cottage, I said,"Where to now? The Amazon rain forest?" Dad said,"There's another horse barn on the other side of Spicer. I think we can get some better horses over there." We both laughed and laughed. He stopped in front of the malt shop in Spicer and we had hot cocoa between the plink, plink, plinks, dripping in the pots and pans set all over the floor of the malt shop. It was a dumb afternoon, but I don't think I'll ever forget it.

July 1 Friday

Getting near the fourth. Jimmy and I rowed over to Spicer and bought some firecrackers. We also bought an 8-inch piece of 1/2 inch pipe, threaded on one end with a cap. We had the plumber drill a small hole in the pipe just below the threads. When we got back we put the cannon on the end of the dock and pointed it out over the lake at a 45 degree angle. We put a firecracker in the threaded end of the pipe, fed the fuse up thru the hole and screwed the cap on tight. Then we put a steely wrapped in a piece of toilet paper to make it a snug fit in the open end, lit the fuse and turned our backs. Always turn your back on the first firing, so if something goes wrong you don't get blinded for life. POW!. It blew the steely about fifty feet out in the lake. So much for inventive genius. We decided to save the rest of the crackers until the 4th.

July 2 Saturday

Played with the diving helmut this afternoon. We had a game going where a guy would put on the helmet and stand on the bottom with air being pumped to him. Then we stopped pumping, and he would see how long he could stay under just breathing the air in the helmet until he gave up or went unconcious. The winner was a girl about our age named Honey. She stayed under 9 minutes. The nearest guy was eight. His name was Stub.

After dark Jimmy and I and his older brother Bob rowed out to a crappie hole just off the point with our fishing poles. We put a flashlight and a couple of rocks in a mason jar and lowered it on a string until it was just off the bottom. Pretty soon there were a dozen crappies poking around the jar. We hung our lines down among them with worms on the hooks and watched them nose around the worms. Whop! One of them took one. We caught 6 apiece. That's the limit for one day.

July 3 Sunday

Jimmy and I thought up a good one for tonight. We broke all our firecrackers in half and emptied the black powder into an empty can with a screw top. We saved all the fuses and tied them end to end until we had a foot long fuse. While we were doing it, Jimmy said he thought we better get another batch of fire crackers, because if we pull this off we don't want people asking us where all our firecrackers went on the morning of the 4th.

So when we finished we hiked over to Spicer and bought a few more firecrackers plus 3 skyrockets. We asked our folks if we could sleep on the grass behind the cottages tonight in our bedrolls. They said ok.

By eleven o'clock most of the cottages were dark. By midnight they were all dark. We shoved the long fuse into the can of powder and buried it in the sand on the beach. Then we stuck the 3 rocket sticks in the sand about ten feet apart pointing out over the lake. We were set. At 12:30 we lit the can of powder fuse. Then ran and lit the 3 rockets and took off for our bedrolls.

First the can went off. KABOOM! and blew a five foot hole in the beach. All the lights in the cottages came on. People ran out to see what happened. Then the 3 rockets took off. Whooosh - Pow..stars all over. What a way to bring in the fourth of July, huh?

July 4 Monday

We packed up early this morning because another family was renting the cottage at noon. While I was waiting around I collected dandelion seeds, the white fuzzy stuff, until I had a ball about the size of a grapefruit. I buried it beside the maple tree in the backyard of our neighbors cottage next door. I'll bet they'll be surprised next spring what a beautiful big plant of dandelions comes up.

I said goodbye to Jimmy and the other kids and gave the crow a zweibach. As we pulled out mom said,"Who do you suppose pulled that stunt last night?" Charlotte said,"It was probably those firemen from Spicer. They always pull practical jokes on the 4th of July." and rolled her eyes up at me. Sisters are kind of handy once in a while.

We got back home about 11. I ran across the alley to see if Fish was still there. He was. We were going to go out to the fourth of July celebration at the fairgrounds together. We were biking along State street eating frozen Snickers I brought out, when we see the biplane overhead. We had almost forgotten about the batman.

We put on speed and pumped up that blankety blank hill again. When we got there the pilot and the stunt man were refueling it again out of the five gallon drum. When they finished the pilot introduced us to Steve, the stunt man. He didn't look like a stunt man. He was short and skinny and had a pimply face. His hand shook so much that his cigarette sent little smoke rings up into the air. Every now and then he'd have a fit of shaking all over. Fish said to him,"Are you ok?" and the pilot answered for him. "Oh, he always shakes like that just before he goes up. Once he jumps he's ok." I thought, How would you know? but I didn't say it.

We watched the guy put on his harness. It was a long sleeved jacket with a piece of canvas sewed along the underside of each arm and along the side of the jacket. There was also a triangular canvas between his legs, so when he spread his arms and legs he became sort of a flying kite. Then the pilot helped him put on a chest pack chute. He couldn't wear a seat pack chute because it dangled around too much while he was gliding around.

Steve got up and started to shake again so bad we had to help him up in the front cockpit, while the pilot started the engine and climbed aboard. We yelled, "Auf Wiedersehn." and away they bounced... a nutty pilot, a smashed instrument panel and a Batman shaking with terror.

Down the hill we tore and over to the fairgrounds. There was a slight west wind blowing, so the Jenny kept about a quarter of a mile west of the fairgrounds, and kept going up and up until it was about 8000 feet up. We could see the batman crawl out on the wing and then off he jumped. He went straight down for a few hundred feet and then spread his arms and legs and zoomed up into a loop, did a few circles and then went into a tuck and somersaulted a few times. Came out of it. Did a few more zooms and figure eights and finally cracked his chute just above the fairgrounds. Fish and I timed him by counting seconds. We figured he was flying around for no more than 20 or 30 seconds, but it seemed like a lot more. Anyhow the chute swung him down running into the baseball diamond right in front of the grandstand. He unhooked his harness in a second and came running up to home plate where he took a bunch of bows to the applause from the grandstand and drums doing a riffle with a big CRASH! at the end. People were saying,"Wow, what nerves of steel that guy must have!"

July 8 Friday

Fish's dad is an interstate truck driver. That's
why he isn't home much. He is big and sort of
tough. I went over to Fish's house this morning,
because we were going to play baseball with the
Goosetown gang out at the park. Fish was
finishing his oatmeal in the kitchen, and his dad
was sitting at the table reading the newspaper.

Suddenly his dad put down the paper and said,
"Richard, I really haven't spent much time with
you the last few years, and I think we ought to get
to know each other better. How would you like to
go fishing over at Lake Hanska?" Fish said, "No. I
want to go play baseball with the gang." His dad
said, "Well, all boys ought to know the outdoors,
so get your butt upstairs and get your fishing
pole." Fish said he didn't have a fishing pole.
That stumped him, so he said, "Well, you can use
mine." He yelled, "Esther, where is my fishing
pole?" Fish's mom yelled back from upstairs, "You
gave it to that bearded guy at the Mormon picnic
three years ago."

"Well," he mumbled, "then we'll go hiking. Go get
your boots on." Fish said he didn't have any boots.
His dad said, "Get in the car. We're going whether
you like it or not." He looked sort of mad, and I
didn't know what to do, so I got in the car with
Fish. We spun gravel for about half a block and
skidded around the corner down fifth north
toward the river. When we got to the bridge
there had been an accident and several cars were
stalled there. A big green Durant was sideways on
the road, blocking the entrance to the bridge. We
stopped and waited for about five minutes while
the drivers of the cars were yelling about
something. After another few minutes, Fish's dad

stuck his head out the window and yelled, "Stop blabbing and back that green hunk of junk off the road, you stupid knuckle head."

This guy gets out of the Durant. He is taller and bigger than Red Grange and has a face that is meaner than a skull. He says in a very even voice. "What...did...you...say?" Fish's dad says, "Oh, not you Sir. I was speaking to that old lady in the Model A over there." Death head gets back in his green Durant. Fish says, "You were sure lucky that Model A was green." His dad said, "Shut up!" Then he turned the car around. We went back home then.

July 9 Saturday

It's green apple time now. We have four apple trees in our back yard, and there are apple trees all over the neighborhood. We guys carry a salt shaker in our back pocket. When we feel hungry we pick a few green apples about the size of a fifty cent piece, sprinkle salt on them and chew away. It's kind of a bitter taste, but no one will admit it, so we keep pretending we enjoy them.

This afternoon we chose sides and had a war. There weren't any rules. You just run around between the garages in the alley and plug the apples as hard as you can at anything that moves. When you get hit square, you know it. Bunny and Babe got in another fight, because Bunny threw three apples at Babe at the same time and one hit him in the mouth. Bunny lost another shirt before we pulled them apart. It's a good thing his dad is a clothing salesman. About 4 o'clock we were all wringing wet and tired of being bruised, so we got our swim suits and biked out to the dam. On the way home Mr.Nelson stopped and let us all get in the back of his hay truck with our bikes and gave us a ride back to town. His daughter is in my class in school.

July 10 Sunday

Fish, JR, Goose and I were shooting arrows at some bales of hay behind Turner Hall when Tom came out and asked if we wanted to go to Lake Crystal. We all called home and climbed into his new Model A Ford sedan with our bows, cuz he said they were having an archery contest there and maybe we could get in it. When we arrived there was a Chataqua celebration going on. Chataquas are sort of ritzy carnivals that travel from town to town. They have singers, musicians, some booths and put on plays in a big tent. They promote the local talent by letting them take parts in the plays or show off their other talents like singing or playing a musical instrument. It's sort of a cooperative arrangement between the Chataqua and the town, with the town sometimes getting a percent of the profit if there is one, etc. Anyhow, they didn't have an archery contest, but they did have an archery range set up with prizes for bull's eyes. They had bows and arrows there, but said we could use our own. You get to shoot three arrows for practice and then you pay 25 cents for three shots that count. The targets were about 50 feet away, so it wasn't like shooting fish in a barrel for us amateurs. Tom shot first and told us what he thought the Kentucky windage was. He shot two golds and won a hip flask. I hit one bull and got a carton of Chesterfields. Fish got a china Dresden doll. Goose and JR got in the red but didn't make the gold.

When we got a little ways away we about died laughing thinking about Tom carrying a hip flask so he could sneak snorts between gym classes. And we pictured me flicking ashes on Harry Daggart's desk when he called me in for being tardy all the time. I traded the Chesterfields to Fish for the Dresden doll cuz his brother smokes. Mom is nuts about figurines. We have a thousand of them all over the house, and guess who has to dust them.

We wandered around a bit and watched some three legged races where they tie the left leg of one person to the right leg of his partner. Also there were races where you have both feet in a gunny sack. Boy, there were some nasty tumbles on that one. The funniest thing of the day was a tug of war between some women that went nowhere.

Each side had a real fat woman on the end of the rope. And when those two gals sat down and dug their heels in the dirt the other team wasn't strong enough to move them. They tugged and tugged and the handkerchief in the middle of the rope never moved either way. Then the girls started to giggle and laugh. Then they stood up and doubled over laughing. Then they'd sober up, grab ahold of the rope and even if the other team wasn't even holding on to the rope they couldn't budge the handkerchief an inch. They tried one last time, but somebody giggled and they all collapsed laughing hysterically. It was so ridiculous even the crowd was in tears laughing. The referee finally made a long flowery speech about stamina, strength, training and the will to win and awarded the prize of a twenty pound ham to the two fat women.

On the way home we pulled a neat trick on Tom. Fish was in the front seat. He had an arrow ready. We were doing about forty when I clapped my hands over Tom's eyes from the back seat. Goose and JR grabbed his arms back against the seat while Fish pushed the gas pedal down with the arrow and steered the car with his other hand. Tom was yelling, "You idiots. You're going to kill us all!!" After a few hundred yards we let him go.

We went to Eibner's when we got back. He made us chip together and buy him a triple chocolate, strawberry, vanilla, banana split with milk chcolate, salted peanuts and marshmallow topping. There went our allowance for the week. We only had twenty cents left so the four of us had to split a 20 cent sundae between us. Tom wouldn't give us any money. He said, we had to learn to suffer for our sins.

He reminded us all to get packed for scout camp tomorrow.

July 17 Sunday

Forgot to write during the week. There was too much to do at camp. In our row of nine tents we got ninth every inspection except Thursday, when we got eighth, because the number 4 blew down. JR brought along his violin. He didn't want to, but one of the counselors pushed him into it. Anyhow we guys got together and pulled a gag on him.

At campfire one night, JR was scheduled to play his violin. Now JR and I have one thing in common; we hate music. His mother forced him to take lessons, and like me, he ended up being able to play only one piece, "Roses of Picardy". And he is lousy, believe me.

Well, he slouched up to the campfire and we all applauded. But as he played one after the other of the scouts would get up and drift out of sight into the dark. JR was busy looking at his music so he didn't notice the entire fire circle was empty. When he finished he looked around and there was nobody there. He stood there looking stupid. Then we all rushed back, picked up JR and threw him off the end of the dock, clothes and all. We did save his violin, however.

I tell you, he'll never live that one down, and I'll bet it'll be a long time before he plays "Roses of Picardy" again. He took it pretty well and laughed with the rest of us. He's always playing jokes on people like shooting us in the legs with his BB gun, so he expects to catch it himself once in a while.

July 24 Sunday

Last week a kid named Jack Jordan and I entered a southern Minnesota tennis tournament at Mankato. Fish and I usually play doubles together, but Fish said he and Winshield had invited two girls to a picnic. I asked him who and he wouldn't tell me. Picnicking before tennis. Ye Gods and little fishes... Are they going soft in the head?

Jack and I went over to Hal's house at 6:30 this morning to drag him out of bed so he'd make the 7 o'clock mass. We lost the last town match we had with a Redwood Falls team by default because he missed early mass. He was ahead one set and 4-2 when he had to quit so we could tear home at 70 miles per hour to get him to the last mass on Sunday evening. We tried to find a priest that played tennis, so we could set up a sort of portable mass deal. The best we could find was an assistant priest, Corky Gedsted, who played Ping Pong, but he couldn't get away on Sundays.

This Sunday was important, because Jack and I had made it to the semi's during the week and were scheduled to meet the Minneapolis - St. Paul public courts champs at 10. They were seeded number one, and we wanted Hal along to coach us. We got there ok and lost the first set 6-3. However, one of our opponents, was a top player in Minnesota. He knew he was good and sort of strutted around bellyaching when he missed a set-up, etc. Also he kept a bottle of Sasparilla by the net post and now and then he'd walk over and take a swig. Now this is perfectly legal as long as you don't delay play, but he was doing it anytime he felt like it. We'd get ready to serve and there he would be standing by the net post drinking. During a break Hal handed Jack a bottle of NEHI orange pop and told him to put it by the other net post. Every time the Champ took a swig, Jack would wait until he got back into position, and then Jack would walk over and take a slug out of his bottle. The audience thought this was pretty funny, but you could see the storm clouds gathering over the Champ's head. He missed a few and we were level at 6-6. Now he started barking commands at his partner, like "Get back! Move! Didn't you see that coming !", Etc. We took our serve and it was 7-6. During the game interval Hal pointed out how much the Champ was poaching and suggested we go for broke and drive the next six returns down the line or right at the Champ.

Now the Champ had been having to stretch for balls for 31 games, because we tried to play his partner every shot. If he wanted to get in the game he had had to start fast for a poach at the net or elbow his partner out of the way to hog a center shot or a lob. Luck was with us. His partner double faulted the first point. C turned, looked at him and stood shaking his head. First serve to me was long. Second serve. I got set as if to drive it cross court as usual, but instead I walloped a flat drive right at C. He muffed it. First service to Jack. C started his drift to poach and Jack drove a top spin down his alley. 40-0. Someone in the gallery giggled. Bless her little ill-mannered heart. C turned and threw his racket against the backstop. That did it. We took the set 8-6 and won the third set 6-2. The Champs partner crumbled in the third set also. There is always a certain security when you have a good partner and you're ahead. But as Tom always taught us kids: Your real game in ANY sport is how well you play when your partner or your team is crumbling and you are behind. That's your real game! Character is how you act during adversity; not how you act when everything is going great.

Well, we got beat that afternoon in the finals, but boy, did we have our moment in the sun plus two nice little bronze medals.

July 31 Sunday

August doldrums coming up... everybody goes on vacation. Dad is taking us up to Lutsen Resort on the north shore of Lake Superior near the end of August, mainly because he and I get hayfever and then asthma about that time. Lutsen usually has a frost by the first of September which knocks out the pollen and we can breathe up there. School starts about September 6, so I'm always two weeks late starting school.

Bunny and Babe have already gone to the Wisconsin Dells for August. Goose is working on his uncle's farm out by Cambria. Fritz's dad is sick, and Fritz has had to stay home a lot to help take care of his two kid sisters. Fish and Windshield are lovesick. They're out all the time with Betty and Nola. Jr's family took him kicking and screaming up to Lake of the Woods so his dad can get some fishing for Muskelunge. JR said it's like a morgue filled with mosquitoes. Just before they left, JR's mother asked if I would take care of their canary, Tweety Bird. I said sure, so they brought the cage over and we hung it in the bay window over the davenport the morning they were pulling out.

Dad was at work and mom was out somewhere when I walked through the living room and there was Spats, our cat, with his mouth full of Tweety Bird. He had evidently climbed up on the back of the davenport and clawed the cage until the door flew open and Tweety flew out and that was that. I tried to get the bird away from him, but no go. He crawled under the davenport. Just then the phone rang. It was JR's sister. She said they were packed and ready to go, and how was Tweety Bird doing? I said, "Just fine. He's singing away like mad." She said, "Isn't that wonderful. Give him all our love." I said, "I certainly will. Have a good trip." I had to keep my hand over the mouthpiece so she wouldn't hear the crunch, crunch from under the davenport."

So Tac and I will be flopping around by ourselves for a while, I guess. Tac said we should go looking for old ladies to help across the street, but there isn't enough traffic to seriously hurt anyone. So Tac suggested we just ride away into the sunset down west Franklin with our heads tucked underneath our arms.

August 2 Tuesday

Our town's generating plant is down by the northwestern depot on first north. It pipes water in from the river through a big eight-inch pipe to the boilers that make steam to run the steam engines that turn the dynamos for the town's electricity.

The town board of directors ok'd a 100 foot by 100-foot concrete slab to be laid next to the plant as a foundation for a new maintenance and storage building. But somebody goofed. They laid the concrete over a hundred feet of the water pipe line, and evidently in the process a bull dozer had bumped the pipe and caused it to crack open and start leaking a week after the slab was poured. Oi, Yoi, Yoi.

The repair job to break open the concrete along the pipe until the leak was uncovered amounted to about 3000 dollars in the news article in the Journal. There was talk around town that Charlie Lingenhog, the plant supervisor, should have caught the mistake before the slab was poured. Dad was grumbling tonight about the fact that the architectual firm and the contractors were the ones to blame for the crack and not Charlie whose duty was to supervise the plant's operation and not construction jobs.

143

I laughed, and said,"Why don't you call the old guy from Spicer with his willow wand. He'd find the leak in a minute..Ha, Ha, Ha." Dad said,, "By God, you're right. I'll give him a ring." He pulls out his little memo book and grabs the phone. I couldn't believe it. I figured he was going soft in the head like Fish. Even mom said,"Herman, are you nuts?" But dad is like a bulldog. Mom complains that all Germans are obstinate and pig headed. Dad hung up and said,"Harry will meet us at the generating plant tomorrow at 2 o'clock. I'll call Charlie at home and tell him we're coming."

Aug. 3 Wednesday

Dad took me along. We walked into the plant at 2:05. I thought that dad was really blowing it this time. I felt kind of scared that Harry was out of his league and dad would get laughed at all over town if the story ever got out about witching for water in these modern times. Yeepers.

Dad introduced Charlie to Harry and said, "Charlie, how'd you like to find out exactly where that leak is?" Charlie said, "If you can, Harry, you'll save the town about 3000 dollars and not to mentioned my much aligned reputation." We walked out to the slab.

Harry had brought along a nickel plated rod about 3 feet long with a brass dial attached to it. He sat on the edge of the slab and took off his shoes and socks. Then he walked out on the slab sort of shuffling along all over the slab holding the rod out in front of him. Suddenly the rod pointed down between his feet, and Harry said,"Here's your leak."

Charlie looked at him sideways, but he marked the spot with a blue crayon just as if he believed the guy. There was sort of a silence.Finally Charlie said,"Why, may I ask, do you take off your shoes and socks?" "Well," said Harry, "when pipes break under slabs such as this, the water can't escape very readily,

144

because the ground has been compacted to four or five times its own density. The pressure thus tends to keep building up near the break until some of the water is gradually forced up into the concrete. As you walk barefoot around the slab you can detect where the slab is cooler than the surrounding areas. Voila'. The leak!"

"I'll be damned," said Charlie, "But what the hell is the rod for?" Harry laughed. "Oh, that's just an advertising gimmick like my willow wand." And he ruffled my hair and winked at me again. "People remember me as that crazy witching well digger when they've long forgotten the name or telephone numbers of other well diggers." "Well, I'll be damned." said Charlie again. "Here's your check for two hundred dollars. You've just saved the town a few thousand bucks, plus my butt to boot. Wonder why I didn't think of that?" Harry said, "Hell, you're an electrical engineer. You don't know a damned thing about magic!" Then we all laughed. Harry is sure a smart business man.

On the way home I asked dad how come he took a chance like that on Harry, when he looked like a dumb idiot when he used his wand at our cottage? Dad said," I saw him wink at you at the cottage, remember? I knew then he was pulling our leg and that I had underestimated him just because he was a local from Spicer. Next day I talked to Mr. Nichols, who's lived there for years. He told me that Harry had several degrees in Hydraulic Engineering and had retired from the Navy Department as a top Oceanographer. I felt he had taken me in and I had fallen for it. So I had to call him and act as if I had known all along and that he really hadn't taken me in. Eh, eh, eh."

Jeez. Adults are really wierd.

Aug. 6 Saturday

Dad took a week off, and he and mom went to Detroit Lakes by themselves at their favorite resort. Jerry is at the U, so Charlotte had to baby sit me for the week. I don't know why, because I can lick her wrestling any day in the week. What good would she be if some tough tried to kidnap me? Anyhow, Charlotte and I made up a letter and sent it to them on Monday.

Dear Mom and Dad,

Everything is going fine. It's 2 a.m. as I write this. I can't get Billy to go to bed, and he's playing with matches in the fireplace. He left the icebox door open last night. I closed it this morning, but something in there smells funny. This afternoon he ran along the top of the back fence with an open scissors in his hand just to see if he could do it. I couldn't stop him.

We left our bicycles in the driveway before supper, tracked some mud into the kitchen and ate supper with our caps on without washing our hands. We ate dessert first and left all the vegetables on our plates. We weren't very hungry anyhow. I had 3 hershey bars at 5 o'clock and Billy ate the lemon pie you left.

I'm sitting next to the radio by the open window with the volume turned up listening to Red Nichols and his Five Pennies. Only two neighbors have called so far to complain.

Well, Billy finally fell asleep on the hearth, but he did get a fire started. I'll just leave him there for the night and go upstairs to bed. We haven't seen Fido for three days.

Love and kisses,

Aug. 7 Sunday

I'm tired of writing again. I think I'll lay off until we get back from Lutsen. I'll be a freshman in high school, with a brand new principal. Whoopee!

x x x x x x x x x x

Sep. 26 Monday

We got home yesterday. At Lutsen everybody had left the resort as soon as school started, so it was pretty quiet, except for one incident.

In front of the stony beach about fifty yards out in the lake is a big rock about 30 feet across and 6 or 7 feet high. Lake Superior was carved out of bedrock by glacier action a few years ago. When you look down in the water, the bottom is full of wierd twisted rock formations and black holes. The water temperature doesn't vary much from 32 degrees winter or summer, so there aren't many people swimming around in it.

This one day I swam out to the rock and laid on it a while to get warm enough to swim back. It was a bright sunny day with no indication of death anywhere. But wait, the plot will unfold before your very bloodshot eyes.

There is a stream that tumbles down from the hills behind Lutsen and empties into the lake just to the north of the rock. I noticed this time there was a beautiful white sandy beach just the other side of the stream mouth, so I thought I'd swim over there. I made a mistake. I didn't realize the amount of water that flows out of a stream that size. I dived off the rock and swam the crawl for a minute or so when I looked up. Ye Gods. I was about 150 yards off shore and the current was carrying me farther out every

147

second. I treaded water a second and estimated I was over half way across so there was no sense in trying to go back. I yelled a few times but there wasn't a soul in sight. I was colder than hell, but I figured the only way out was to swim like mad, get past the outflow and then make for shore. I kept swimming, but my arms were getting stiff and my legs were numb. I'd been in the water close to ten minutes when I got across the current, but I still had 300 yards to go to get back to shore. I made it ok, but by that time I was so stiff and numb I couldn't stand up. I dragged myself out of the water on my elbows and laid there in the sun until I thawed out. That was a close one. No wonder Tom always told us to swim with a buddy. Br-rr-rr.

I took off for school this morning. Mom said that Dr. Andresen had retired last year and there would be a new principal at the high school. On the way there was a cement truck with some guys laying and repairing a sidewalk by Turner Hall. I guess I got carried away watching, and then I counted the squares in the sidewalk in the next block and figured out how many cubic yards of concrete it would take to lay a block of sidewalk. This took some figuring. When I got to school nobody was around. Late the first day. I considered going home and giving it a try Tuesday but figured I was new, crippled with asthma and with a new principal that didn't know me, it should be a shoo in.

I entered the front door and climbed the stairs to the second floor where the administrative offices and classrooms were. I started down the hall when a student monitor stopped me and said, "Where's your hall pass?" I told him I didn't have one. He said, "What are you doing out of class?" I said, "I haven't been in class." That stumped him. "What are you doing in the hall?" I said, "I'm going to assasinate the principal. Where is his office?" He said, "Right down the hall. End door." I stopped in front of the door

and practiced a few asthmatic coughs. I knocked. A
voice said, "Come in." I went in bent way over with a
spasm of coughing. The voice said,"It won't work.
You pulled that last year." I looked up. Ye Gods, there
was Harry Daggart sitting behind a big desk. He said,
"What's the excuse this time. Been counting the
chickens?" I said, "No Sir, but I have been counting
the squares in the sidewalk." He said, "Oh, then it's
alright. And here's your schedule: English,
U.S.History Latin I and either arithmetic or algebra I.
Do you think you can handle algebra?" I said, "Yes
Sir, I'm pretty good at arithmetic already. Let me
show you."

I noticed there were a few notes written on his desk
memo pad, so I tore off the top sheet and carried
the pad over beside him. I took his fountain pen out
of his pocket and wrote out my calculations
regarding the 13 cubic yards of concrete necessary
for a block of sidewalk. I put the pen back in his
shirt pocket and said, "What do you think?" He
sighed and said, "Algebra it is then. Room 114. Miss
Treadwell." I stood there. He said, "Now." I turned at
the door and said, "Thank you." He didn't answer. He
was staring down at his shirt pocket where a purple
stain was spreading across his shirt front. Ye Gods. I
had forgotten to put the cap on his fountain pen!

After school I walked down to Schroeder's Bakery and bought two raised donuts for a nickel. Then I walked over to the junior high to see if I could catch some of the gang. Tac was playing mumbledepeg with two other kids, but nobody else was around. I watched a while. Then I asked Tac where the guys were. He said that since school started some of them had been shoving off right after school was out. I walked on home along State Street, when Fritz came by on his bike with a bunch of groceries in his basket. He stopped and we gabbed a while about what we'd done during the summer. When he got ready to go, he said, "You know we're moving to Minneapolis?" I said, "No. How come? Your dad get a new job down there?" He said, "No. Dad died last month. Didn't you hear?" I said, "Gosh no, Fritz, I'm sorry." He said, "Well, mom's brother and some of her family live there, so they'd be helping us out while I...." I could see he was near tears, so I cut him off short and said, "Well, we get down there often. Send me a card with your address and I'll come see you. Ok?" He said, "Will do. And avoirdupois to you, Billy Billy Beaner, Beckhouse Cleaner." And off he pedalled waving one hand in the air. Then I felt like bawling.

Sep. 28 Wednesday

I was looking out the window in English class when a monitor came in and gave a slip of paper to Miss Ritter. She said, "Billy, will you please report to the principal's office?" I said, "I'd rather not." The whole class laughed. She said, "Go!" I said, "You know, it's not fair." She said, "What's not fair?" I said, "Well, when my dad goes to a meeting he knows why he's going. When you teachers are called in, you know why you're going. When we are called in we never know whether it's a warrant out for our arrest, whether our house burned down or whether our mother just died from uremic poisoning."

Several kids said, "Yeah. He's right." Then Miss Ritter said, "Well, I can tell you one thing. It's not because of the purple shirt. I think he wants to talk to you about a Phys-Ed class." I said, Thanks, Miss Ritter you're great." Sure enough, Harry only wanted to know whether I wanted to take gym or football. He didn't say anything about the shirt. I thought, well, I might as well try football. I'm not to hot at anything else. That was another mistake. It was like telling yourself you play the violin equally well with either hand.

Sep. 29 Thursday

After school I reported to the locker room and the coach dug out some equipment for me while the other guys were getting dressed. They looked bigger naked than I did dressed. I had forgotten I needed a jockey strap, so I wore my underwear shorts instead, figuring the way the pants smelled, an ounce of prevention was worth a pound of cure for the least of which would be the King's Evil. There were no knee pads in the pants, and how was I to know you had to bring your own woolen socks. So between the canvas flaps hanging down over my knees and my black socks hanging down over the gunboats on my feet were my white shinbones. The jersey I got was black. All the other guys had purple and white, the school colors. It did go with my socks, however. My helmet was a marvel of engineering circa 1912. If Wilbur Wright had worn it on his first flight it probably was the reason he got off the ground at all. The ear flaps stuck straight out from the leather cap. With genius born of desperation I found an old wet shoelace in the shower and made a chin strap.

Then we all clumped out as loud as we could across the wooden floors to a flatbed truck and sat around the edge. On the way to the fairgrounds where we practiced we'd all yell at the girls on the way home from school.

We got out to the football field and went through warm-up exercises. There were 17 guys out for football. There are 240 students in the high school and 120 of them are boys. One hundred and three of them were smarter than me.

We started to scrimmage. The first team would line up to run a play around right end. So they'd put us Four Horsemen of Notre Dame, opposite the right side of their line with the two other guys as defensive backs behind us, and then run the play several times. Then they'd switch us to the other side and run the off tackle and end runs on that side. He put me at end. I was supposed to turn the play in toward the tackle and guard. I think they always put the thin scrawny guys at end because there's no other place to put them. On the first play I see these 3 guys running interference coming right at me.

(I must interject a note here in self defense of my coming actions. The first team players are mostly Juniors and Seniors. I had skipped the second grade. So statistically I am an eighth grader. That makes these guys 3 or 4 years older than me, and they are the biggest of the lot. Also, if Achilles had the armor I had on he would have fled in terror.)

When they got to me I laid down sideways. They were so surprised they stumbled over me, and the guy carrying the ball ran into them, fell down and lost a yard. The coach didn't compliment me. He just yelled at the backfield. "Come on now. Are you guys going to let a Freshman throw you for a loss? I want to see you run over him!" Here they come again. This time I ran over and hid behind the two tackles lurching each other around. The interference thundered on by looking for the end and I caught the ball carrier as he went by. He only made two yards. But I was out of options.

Sep. 30 Friday

Football: Day two.

Today one of those unsung heroes kept me from
being maldeformed the rest of my life. Elmer Marks
was the best running back we had. He had bow legs
like pistons. And I've seen him run over two guys at a
time. I was playing defensive back, when he broke
through the line and came right at me. I hit him
with my shoulder and expected to get knocked flat,
but I felt him relax and down he went. It took me a
couple of seconds, but all of a sudden it hit me. He
didn't want to hurt me. And he evidently wanted me
to look good or he would have run around me with
ease. You never know who people really are, do you?

I signed up for gym, where I belonged, on Monday.
There aren't too many Elmer Marks's playing
football.

Oct. 8 Saturday

Outside of town on the road to Mankato next to the
river bank, a new night club is opening called "The
Black Dragon." The owner, Mr. Block, is a member of
the Chamber of Commerce and had seen Loyd and I
do that balcony scene at Turner Hall. He got a hold of
Ernie Herrigan and asked if we would do a gag for
him on opening night at the peak of the dining hour
at the Black Dragon. We said sure.

This time I got dressed up like a little old lady with a
wig and big hat, so nobody could tell who it was, and
sat in this old wheel chair. Loyd dressed up in a suit
and tie with fake mustache to look older, and as
neither of us hang around bars or night clubs much,
none of the diners were apt to recognize us anyhow.

Outside the Dragon entrance is a long wooden walkway down to a dock sticking out into the river where boats sometimes tie up. A few overhead lights are nailed to 2 by 4's sticking up from the railings. At nine o'clock the dining room is packed. It is almost dark when Loyd wheels me into the dining room area. We wait by the door waiting to be seated, but after a few minues the old lady starts to complain mildly at first then louder and louder about not getting any attention. Finally Mr. Block comes over. He's in on all this, and I bawl him out rather loudly, and Loyd tries to shush me. By this time everyone in the dining room is watching this raucous old biddy. Loyd tries to calm me down but to no avail. When Block shows us a table by the kitchen door I really raise cain telling him loudly it's an insult to seat a crippled old lady by the garbage cans. Mr. Block assures me he will find me another table. I continue to rant and rave, and at this point Loyd throws his hands in the air, and yells, "That's it. I've had it. Now you ill-mannered old biddy, I'm going to shut you up permanently!"

With that he wheels me out the entrance and pushes the wheelchair at a dead run down the walkway until about twenty feet from the end of the dock he gives me a final shove The wheelchair with me in it goes sailing off the end of the dock kersplash into the river My hat goes floating down the river while I grab a big breath and swim under water back under the dock lugging the wheelchair behind me Loyd in the meantime walks briskly up the walkway shaking his head and disappears into the darkness of the parking lot

You never saw such turmoil Everybody had rushed to the windows to watch the murder take place under the dim arc lights Some of the younger men started running down the walkway to save me but Mr Block had foreseen this and blocked their way by whispering Its a gag Its a gag So the guys just stood there looking down into the muddy waters shaking their heads to go with the gag

Well Mr Block persuaded the customers to go back to their tables and announced that the sheriff had been notified and there was nothing to be done until they got here anyhow Things finally settled down A few minutes later Loyd and I walked in the entrance with me still dripping wet and as everybody turned we bowed and Mr Block announced Ladies and Gentlemen this is the beginning of tonights entertainment and a pleasant dinner to you all

The customers were flabbergasted What a preformance That story went around town for days The New Ulm Review even printed the story on their front page with the head MURDER AT THE BLACK DRAGON Mr Block is a sharp business man

Oct. 10 Monday

Today we had a real young substitute teacher in English. She was sure pretty. She had black hair in a boyish bob with straight bangs across her forehead like Clara Bow, but she had a bigger mouth. She told us Miss Ritter had asked her to review the punctuation marks with us today.

She said, "Did you know that in some ancient languages the words were run together without spacing or punctuation?" No, we didn't know. Well, that was one of the reasons it proved so difficult to translate them into the modern languages.

Then she said we would pretend our class was an ancient Egyptian committee that has been given the task of inventing marks that would help us understand these run together languages. "Now", she said,"we don't want to waste much time making these marks when we are writing, so what's the quickest mark you can make?" A dot, somebody said. Ok she said, what's the next quickest? Comma. Anyhow after a while we ended up with a list of period, comma, apostrophe, question mark,etc.

We used another half hour to decide to use the period to end the sentence; the comma to indicate a minor pause; the semi-colon a major pause and a colon a screeching halt before we hit the next clump of words, etc. She was sharp in getting us to invent the marks, which meant we'd probably never forget them, instead of trying to memorize the dumb things that somebody else had invented.

Then I said,"Actually you don't need the period." She said, "Why not?" I said, "Well, the next sentence always starts with a capital letter. So obviously the sentence before it is done. Why waste time putting in the period?" She said,"Ok, let's get rid of the period." Anybody else? (My God, I thought she was going to tell me that tradition was tradition and that was that!) Nobody said anything. So I said, "Forget all the rest of 'em too." She said, "Explain." "Well," I said, "When we talk,(comma) we don't (with apostrophe) use punctuation marks, (comma) such as: (colon) quotation marks (comma) and so forth." (period) (quotation marks). "So why not forget them in writing?"(question mark) (quotation marks).

She said, "Quotation marks, Any rebuttals? question mark, quotation marks." and grinned. Laura, sitting next to me, quick as a flash, says, "Quotation marks, He's Apostrophe, right. Period. Let's , apostrophe, throw them all out the window. Period. Quotation marks." The bell rang. Clara Bow-two, said,"As chairman of our committee, I agree. I will report to Miss Ritter that our Egyptian advisory committee has decided that puncuation marks have become useless now that people read so fast. And we don't have to worry about them any more!" Then she laughed and laughed.

Look at the last 3 paragraphs of Saturday, October 8. I didn't use any punctuation marks. I'll bet you didn't even miss them.

As we walked out she motioned me over to her desk. "That's the way to think, you know." she said. "Challenge the principles. Don't accept everything just because it's printed in a book or been done for thousand of years. Keep it up, kid. Somebody like you only comes along once in a blue moon. Good luck." I thanked her and went on out. Fish was waiting for me in the hall and wanted to know what she wanted. I said, "She asked me for a date tonight." Fish pulled my shirt out of my pants. She is just like Jim Becher. I wish they could meet each other. They make you believe in yourself, and your own brain, instead of always giving you C's and pointing out how dumb you are for not being able to memorize everything else in the world.

Oct. 15 Saturday

Jerry was home for the weekend and asked if I wanted to go duck hunting this morning over to Lake Hanska. I said sure. We got up in the dark at 3:30. What fun. He made two sandwiches; put hot coffee in a Thermos; picked up Ernie and drove us out to the blind on a point at the lake just about the time my eyelids came unglued. We climbed a barbed wire fence and squished thru the mud out to the point. I had run ahead, and when I got to the blind, which is an old metal horse watering trough sunk in the marsh with cattails around it, I see 6 ducks bobbing up and down in the water. I raised my shotgun slowly, gave 'em both barrels, and sat down in the mud. A 12 gauge has some kick. The ducks kept right on bobbing.

Jerry came up and told me I had just slaughtered 6 innocent decoys illegally yet. You can't shoot ducks sitting on the water. There I went again, rushing in where angels would have stayed in bed. So I went over and jumped in the blind on top of two beavers. You never heard so much gnashing of buck teeth and flapping of tails in your life. I bounced right out. Anyhow we laid two old fence posts down in and stood back until two of the skinniest beavers you never saw climbed out and staggered down toward the water. We finally got in the blind and sat on some wooden ammunition boxes. Just as the sun came up a lone mallard came flying down the middle of the lake. We could hear the guns going off before he got to us. Bang for the .410's; BAM for the 12 guages, and just across the lake, KABOOM for a 10 guage. The KABOOM boosted that duck up about four feet, but he kept right on flapping down the lake.

Jerry said that the charge went under him and blew him upwards. That most hunters don't realize that you not only have to lead a duck, but you have to aim a little higher than the line of flight, because gravity is pulling your charge down at 16 feet per second. If the charge takes only a quarter of a second to get to the duck, that's about a four foot drop, unless you're shooting straight up. Ernie said, "Let Billy take a crack at the next flight. At least he'll get in one shot today."

Five minutes later along comes a flight of six. I stood up, led the leader, like Jerry said and BAM, the leader went fluttering down; hit the water and sat there looking around. My first thought was,"What did I do that for?" Jerry said, "Take the duck boat and go get it. We don't like to leave a wounded duck." I squished down to the boat, turned it over, put the little oars between the wood pegs and shoved off bent on murder. I got there, reached for the duck, but he fluttered away about 15 feet. I rowed after him and reached again. He looked at me piteously and struggled on again. I kept zig-zagging him toward shore until about 30 feet from shore he made one last flutter, got airborne and flew splat right into an old dead tree where he sort of hung draped over a branch. I beached my landing craft, charged up the beach midst exploding mines and mortar shells and shinneyed up the tree. Just then the 10 guage from across the isthmus yells. "Ernie, get that damn idiot back in the blind. He's scaring away every duck between here and Duluth!" I thanked him under my breath and climbed down. The cerse of civilization had struck again. Two starving beavers, six shattered decoys and a peasant in a bare tree.

Oct. 22 Saturday

This noon Loyd and I were working out in the Turner Hall gym. Loyd was helping me learn an inlocate, which is the reverse of a dislocate on the rings. Now the rings are attached to the ceiling too close to one wall, so on the back swing, the rings swing over the steps leading up to the card room. We put four mats over the steps so I wouldn't get a washboard back if I dropped, and he stood halfway up the stairs to spot me if I lost my grip. You get a good swing going; do a downbeat and a front roll into an inverted hang on the backswing. To get there you have to spread the rings apart while you roll. If you don't time it just right your body weight comes down pretty hard; tears your grip away and you drop.

I did the first two ok, but on the third I was late rolling, and I felt my fingers pulling away. Because I was past the end of the swing and starting back, Loyd thought I was ok and relaxed. When I dropped he managed to dive at me and slap my head out from under me. So I sort of lit on my right shoulder, saw a few stars and rolled down the steps, klunk, on to the gym floor. I sat down on the mats and watched the gym rotate on its Y axis for two minutes. Then I stood up and watched it rotate on the X axis for another two minutes. We decided to call it quits for the day.

159

When we went out, I said to Loyd. "I know I got back to school late, and I've been out for football after school. But where is everybody?" Loyd said, "This summer some of the gang fixed up a sort of clubhouse in that old barn behind Prom's house. They're over there most of the time." I said, "Well, let's go over and see what it looks like." He said, "Ok, but..." I said,"But what?" He said,"Oh, alright, let's go. I haven't seen it either." We walked down Washington Street and then down fourth south to the alley behind the barn. The barn door had a door in it painted bright red. It looked sharp. I opened the door and looked in. There was quite a bit of scurrying around. Four of my gang were there and two kids from the north side of town. They were trying to hide their cigarettes. Why, I don't know, because the room was full of smoke. One of the northsiders said,"Don't you ever knock?" I said,"Not usually when I enter a barn. How are you guys?" Sort of a silence. They had the place fixed up pretty neat. Posters on the wall. Some old car robes spread over a couch; a couple of chairs and a row of peach crates with pillows on them. We went in and sat on the crates.

I said,"I haven't seen you guys since we spent time together in the rehabilitation ward at the St. Cloud reformatory. Whatcha been doing?" Another pause. Finally one of the guys said,"Well, we fixed this place up." Then one of the northsiders asked if we wanted a drink and held up a pint of whiskey. I said, "No thanks. It's too early in the afternoon. How about a Pink Lady later?" Nobody even smiled. I kept on, "How's the Model T?" "Oh, I don't know. It stopped running and nobody wanted to pull the engine again."

Silence. "Did you guys play much tennis over the summer?" I asked, all smiles. "No, not much." Silence. There we sat. I suddenly realized we weren't wanted. We were intruders in this private club. It was a tough pill to swallow. It wasn't as if I had burned their house down and eloped with their 15 year old sister. They were plain, ill-mannered bores. I said, "Let's go, Loyd." And out we went. No goodbyes.

We walked back to our house and got out two frozen Snickers. I felt terrible. Friends and fun three months ago and now I was out, period. I said, "Now I know what you meant by "but". Loyd nodded. I said,"But what the hell is the matter with them? Is it me?" Loyd said,"I learned it the same hard way last year. If you don't smoke or drink, you are not IN, and you might as well get used to it, unless you want to go along with 'em." "But," I said, "I don't care whether they drink or smoke or pick their nose. Why are they so uptight if I DON'T smoke or DON"T drink or DON'T pick my nose? That's just stupid!" Loyd said, "Yup."

We sat a few minutes, and then Loyd said,"I wonder why they think they're so special sitting in a smoke filled box and drinking? Who can't do that?" Then we both started to laugh. I said,"I just can't figure it out either, but 'Goodbye Gang, The End of an Era' would make a great movie title." We talked about it for a while and finally I felt better. Loyd said he was glad it happened to me, cuz he'd been all alone for almost a year. That was why he started hanging out with us younger guys, and he was getting to think that maybe he was wrong. Not much of a silver lining to this one. I guess it was the worst thing that has ever happened to me.

Oct. 27 Thursday

Today sure made up for last Saturday. When the study hall teacher wasn't looking, I kept moving from desk to desk until I got a few desks behind Gretchen. When the bell rang I got behind her walking down the aisle and poked her in the back. She said,"Hi, Bill." without even turning around. I said, "How did you know it was me?" She said, "I saw you desk hopping over to this aisle." I said, "Oh. Can I carry your books?" She said, "I don't have any." Then she added,"But I've got a few in my locker. We could stop there." We walked down the hall to her locker. She took out her notebook; gave me two books and I walked her to her history classroom. I was trying to think of something brilliant to say. My mind was a blank. Then I had an inspiration: "Did you know Fish and I are planning to rob the Citizen's State Bank tomorrow?" "Really?" she said, "My dad is getting me a pet elephant tomorrow too. Isn't that a coincidence? What do you think you'll get?" I said,"Probably twenty years." She said, "No. I mean money." I said, "That depends on how long Mr. Abernathy can hold out the safe combination when we drive bamboo sprouts under his fingernails." We reached the history classroom.

So far so good. I never realized girls could be that fast on the uptake. When she reached for the handle I thought, My God. I'm supposed to open the door for her! I went for the handle and beat her to it. I yanked it open and hit her in the forehead. She staggered back and said, "Thanks." I said, "You don't want to go to the movies with me tomorrow night, do you?" She said, "Yes, I do. What time do you want to pick me up?" I said, "Jeez, I don't know." She said, "The first feature starts at 7:30. How about 7 o'clock?" I said, "That's fine." Then she gives me that smile and goes in the room. I'm still standing there a minute later when she comes out and takes her two books. I get another smile. Her eyes are brown. Her big brother won the hundred in the District Track Meet last year. She is the only girl in school that can do a back flip and then a front flip after a roundoff.

Oct. 28 Friday

Dad had one of his trucks bring up about 30 Basswood packing boxes. Boy! After school Fish, Windshield, Tac and I arranged them in sort of a maze and laid some old blankets and canvas over the top. When the sun shone thru the sides and the knots it made a beautiful golden light inside. So then we piled them up to make higher walls like a small chapel.

Then we started climbing up the outside and daring each other to see who would jump off the highest box. After a few jumps I decided to try the top box, so I climbed all the way up, but when I looked down it looked three times higher than when I looked up. I felt I shouldn't jump, but I couldn't climb back down with the guys watching me. So I shoved off. I probably would have been alright, but my heel caught on the box below me, and I took a half header, landing sort of on my knees and right arm. Boy, did that hurt. I rolled over groaning. Tac said, "You win. I'm glad I didn't."

I went in and laid down on the davenport. Mom called Doc Howard, who happened to be home. (He lives next door.) He felt around, asked me to move my fingers and arm, etc. He asked mom for a big dishtowel and made me a triangle sling just like in the Boy Scout Handbook. He said, "It's probably only a sprain but keep the sling on for a few days until it heals up a bit." When I told him how it happened he said, "I'll give you a piece of advice here. Whenever your body says, 'NO, don't try it!' DON'T. Your brain has a pretty good idea of what you are capable of doing at any age. So listen to it. Of course if your best girl is watching, Go For It" Then he laughed and told mom he wouldn't charge her for the house call if he could stay for supper. Eh, eh.

Oct. 31 Monday

Went to school. Everybody asked me what happened. I had three stories ready: I was testing out a batman's suit from the top of the town water tower when one of the canvas wings tore loose; I was breaking in a bronco out on Nelson's farm when it rammed into the fence and threw me over its head; I got in a fight with two Wallahi guys who were picking on a little kid. One of them tried to kill me with a baseball bat, but I wrested it away from him and drove them off.

When I told the girls they would say, "My goodness, I didn't know you were training to be a batman," or "You really break in horses?" However, when Gretchen came up and looked me in the eye, I told her I jumped off a pile of boxes, caught my heel, like a oaf, and lit on my elbow. She said she was sorry. But then I said, "The boxes were piled eighty feet high. On the way down I went into a tuck, did two somersaults and hit the ground rolling, which probably saved my life." She looked at me sideways and sort of sighed.

Nov. 1 Tuesday

Today was IQ testing day. We have to take multiple choice tests, a Miller Analogy Test and some other math and spelling tests. It took all morning. Harry said we could leave when we finished. I wanted to walk Gretchen home, so I kept watching her and counted the pages she turned so I'd know when she was about to finish. When she got to the thirtieth page, which was the last page, I was on the twenty seventh, so I tore thru the last pages answering everything I knew and then went back and guessed at the rest. As she got up to hand in her test I filled in the last ten answers at full throttle random. We were the first two to hand in the test. As we handed in the papers, Harry looked at me and then at Gretchen and then he gave me a half wink. He is the only person I know who can read minds. I probably compromised my college future and ended up with a 90 IQ, but anyhow, I got to walk her home.

Mom and dad said this evening I was becoming a pretty good writer probably because I wrote a lot, and you can't beat intensive practice. However, I told them I thought I'd pocket my prolific, peripatetic pen. Miss Ritter would say that was alliteration. Fish would say I was putting on the dog. Anyhow, I want to do a few other things. Gretchen likes to play tennis too.

Then dad said, "You know you've kept your diary for a year now. What say you and I go back over it and, just for fun, list all the people who helped you a bit during that year. I call them heroes, because in the long run they are the ones that really count in your life, Bill." So we did. Here's the list.

Miss Christensen

Instead of being irritated at my not practising "The Little Elfin's March", she asked me what piece I would like to learn. Even though I selected one of the toughest pieces to play in the history of piano ragtime, she, undaunted, set about teaching me and succeeded. What a neat lady. She taught me something about understanding.

Henrietta Gorsham

As kids we thought it was fun to make her mad by throwing stuff on her roof. But that day she dumped her box of rocks in the garbage can without saying a word, she taught all of us kids a bit about forgiveness. Dad pointed out that having fun at somebody else's expense can be hell for them.

Tom Fender

Taught me chess, fencing, archery, gymnastics, volleyball and scouting. He laughed at everything. And everything he taught he seemed to be an expert at. He had dates galore but never did have time to get married. He said he had too many kids to bring up already! Then he'd laugh. He exuded confidence and humor. He was an instant buddy with every person he met from shy scared kids in the first day of gym class to the vice president of the United State. Who, incidently, awarded Tom the Siver Beaver which is one of the highest scouting awards given. Tom claimed that the real test of character was how well you acted during adversity; not how you acted when everything was going great. I'll never forget that one.

Doc Howard

One of the few doctors in a small town, he went day and night and weekends. I know, because he lived next door, and his bedroom window was opposite mine. I'd hear his phone ring in the middle of the night, and off he'd go. It wasn't until dad and I talked about him that I realized what dedication to humanity was. We agreed that he should have paced himself a bit more.

Dubby, Dubby Dobrens

The hospital janitor probably saved me from freezing to death in that clothes chute. Dad pointed out that his chasing us off the hospital lawn when we made too much noise was his job, not his personality. You can't judge a person's personality necessarily by the job they have to do.

Red Pink

Station Master. Gave us the old boards from the depot to build our hockey rink sideboards, plus a place to store them during summer

Gooses Father

Took Sunday off to drive us down to the depot and helped supervise the building of the hockey rink.

Old Mrs. Stuse

Didn't want the firemen to know they'd run over Rags, because it would make them sad. Why worry now about whose fault it was. More of us could remember that philosophy. Also made great cookies.

Mrs. Haeberle

Let us use her empty lot for our dirt tennis court. Pointed out that our homemade rackets were better to help us learn to hit the ball in the middle of the strings than regular rackets. Encouraged our creativity and resourcefulness.

Booby Hatch

Laughed at our Herman's hotfoot and suggested we leave well enough alone and go home before we got into trouble.

Poik Schuman

Donated that bag of feathers. Warned us with humor, about slaughter not being a drawing room occupation. "Yah, boys, everybody wants their steaks and bacon but don't want to know anything about killing the animals!"

Ossified Boy and Nurse

The tears of the nurse and the stoicism of Charles
facing certain death after years of torturous living,
certainly brought home to all of us kids how
precious our own health was. Count your blessings
more often.

Doc Hammermeister

Retired, but still helping out in emergencies for free.
He played Capture the Flag once too.

Two Maintenance Men

Gave up their Saturday afternoon to get JR out of that
tar barrel. Instead of griping they laughed about the
whole thing. "But look, kids, please don't pull this
off again on our days off."

Airplane Pilot and Batman

Two of the early barnstormers. One flying by the
seat of his pants without instruments, and the other
shaking with fright but still going through his act.
Behind those "nerves of steel" there sometimes can
be abject terror. We ordinary mortals are not alone.

Ernie Herrigan

He got us those death defying acts and in the duck
blind he made sure I got in at least one shot that day.

Herb Hackbart

Policeman with humor. Also a scoutmaster and
knew the name of every kid in town and usually
where they lived.

Circus Roustabouts

Gave us kids jobs and free tickets. I'm certain the circus would have been put up without us kids. Behind those tough, raucous exteriors were some pretty soft-hearted guys.

Hank Crane

His P-sssst on the graduation stage got me a chair in spite of the holocaust it caused.

JR's dad and Heine Samson

Helped Pete Stern keep his son and home.

Winshield's dad

Pointed out that being right doesn't insure you'll be praised. That having character is often a very lonely job. But there is no alternative. You have to believe in yourself come hell or highwater.

Judge Gislason

Invited us young kids to his chess club. Had volumes of chess books and would demonstrate a new opening or variation to us each time we met. He alone of all the men in the chess club had the capacity to play us at our level and teach us something about attack or defense every time we played him. A brilliant guy who loved to challenge us. He always seemed delighted when we showed up on those chess evenings. A real teacher.

Jimmy's Uncle

I never met him but he came through with a Chevy windshield and four old Chevy tires for our Model T.

Charlotte

Big sister. A driver. An exponent of women's rights from the word go. Took a Model T across the west to California and back with two other girls. Kept their hair tucked under their caps, fixed their own engine troubles, changed umpteen tires, and made it halfway back until the T gave up the ghost in the middle of South Dakota. She always griped about the sissy way girl's basketball was played. The court was divided into 3 parts; the guards in the back court, centers in the center section and the forwards in the forward court. She thought bloomers were stupid and wanted to wear shorts ten years before society allowed. Shorts finally did come in at the same time men were allowed on public beaches without tops on their swim suits. Year: 1934. First one in town to get her hair bobbed. Taught me not to be one of the sheep. One spring we guys had been swimming in the Cottonwood River by breaking the ice out, which was strictly against family rules and common sense besides. I asked Charlotte if she thought I should tell mother and dad. Her answer was, "Are you crazy?"

Jim Becher

He believed that training was being told what other people had learned, but that education was learning what to do with your curiosity. By using the Socrates method of asking questions instead of having us memorize answers, he taught us to discuss and think out a solution on our own. He also made certain that we practiced an act of kindness (Henrietta's tree) after we had concluded that kindness was the prime requisite of any religion. Dad said that one bit of religious philosophy was the most important single idea in the world! Wow! And we kids thought that up? I would never have thought of that, but it's hard to think of a better one. Can you?

Miss Stolz

When the Christmas program turned into a bedlam of laughter she didn't panic. Even though we had blown the manger scene into bits, she didn't lay the blame on us. In fact she complimented us three idiots later; she wasn't about to send three kids home from a Christmas program feeling like criminals. To heck with her play and her reputation at the moment. She saw the real meaning of Christmas even through the chaos, confusion and guffaws. What a lady. She had guts!

Hal Soukup, Ed Hagen, Stanley Fremgard, Donald Dannheim

All college boys who helped us learn tennis, hockey, building radios or just giving us a lift somewhere. Amazing how some guys, like these, always seem to be helping others. The news media keeps wondering where the heroes or role models are for modern youth. Heck, all you have to do is look around you.

Jerry

Big brother. "Forget the facts, Willy. Learn the principles." Besides teaching me a jab and a right cross, there were a couple of phrases regarding optimism in life: "Well, it's a lot better than a kick in the butt with a hobnailed boot." or "Better than a jab in the eye with a pointed stick." and a few others that are too vulgar to print.

Clara Bow II

"Challenge the principles, kid; somebody like you only comes along once in a blue moon." That one remark has kept my head above water many a time. Thanks.

Cuggy Nieman

Taking time to drop over and make certain we'd get the Model T running. Obviously dug into his own pocket to get those magneto parts for us.

Elmer Marks

The star of the football team takes it easy on the kid. Not too many high school players would ever think compassion in practice against rookies three years younger than they were. Dad pointed out that Elmer was the youngest of the heroes we were listing, and that that was pretty amazing. Well, maybe not. As Jim pointed out, real heroes are just built that way. They do it because they want to and really never get noticed very much.

THE END

EPILOGUE

Mom said that now that I finished my "Diry", I ought to put in some statistics about the years during which I wrote. Then when I read it in later years the information would help me recall the times in which I lived as a boy. So here are some about 1929.

U.S. population   125,000,000
Stock Market Crash -1929- 20% unemployed.
Two thirds of the population had incomes under $1500 a year.
No income tax on incomes under $3000.
Couple earning $4000/yr. income tax was $8.
Top incomes, such as those for lawyers or doctors, were $5000 on which the income tax was $80.
Postage stamps were 3 cents.
Gallon of gasoline, 15 cents.
Movies cost 10 cents for kids under twelve.
One in eight people had a telephone.
Most rural home used kerosene lamps
Hudson cars cost $890.
Ten percent of smokers rolled their own.
Candy bars were a nickel: Baby Ruth, Snickers and Three Musketeers were the big sellers.
Maids made $5/week; worked 60 hours a week.
Thirty percent of the population had a high school diploma.
Ten percent of college age youth were in college.

Half the farmers were tenant farmers or sharecroppers, tilling someone else's land; eating corn bread and beans; making clothes out of flour sacks and going further in debt each year. Gangs of men were hijacking produce trucks on the way to the cities for food for their families. Anarchy was just around the corner.

173

Tuberculosis, scarlet fever, pneumonia and the flu killed people by the thousands.
Diptheria, measels and whooping cough killed children by the thousands.
Rotten teeth were the rule; not the exception.

Eighty percent of the population felt the government should provide health care for those who couldn't afford it.
The majority felt that owners of guns should register them with the government.
Majority of whites polled felt that there should be separate schools, restaurants and neighborhoods for Negroes.

Thirteen million Negroes were denied the right to vote.
Fifty aging four-stack destroyers were offered for scrap at $5000 apiece.
America's military force was ranked twentieth in the world. Portugal was 19th.

RADIO SCRIPT

Ending the last episode of Jack Armstrong, the All American Boy, and fun-loving Billy Fairchild in "Search for Uranium". They have foiled the mad doctor, Shupato, and uncovered the valuable uranium deposit on the mysterious island of Kur. Now they are rowing out to Uncle Jim's Yacht, "Spindrift", that rides at anchor in the warm waters of the Sulu Sea.

Splashing noises and oarlock creaks.

Billy: Jumpin-Jiminy, Yikes, Jack, we're going to be famous!
Jack: Quiet, Billy, there's no time for that now. If we can get that uranium for the scientists at Hudson High, we"ll probably learn how to make energy from the atom. And then we'll use it for the good of the whole world.
Billy: You're right, Jack.
Jack: Billy, when I think of this country of ours with millions of homes and families stretching from sea to sea and with everybody working and pulling together to have a nation where everybody can be free and happy and do great, fine things ... why it makes me realize what a terrible important job we've got ahead.
There's Uncle Jim on the foredeck.

"Ahoy there, Uncle Jim. We're all ok."

"Our business in life is not to succeed but to continue to fail in good spirits."

Robert "Louie" Stevenson
Scholar Emeritus

"If you fail, remembr that most peeple can't do anything eether."

Billy Billy Beaner
Backhouse Cleaner